STUDENT COOKBOOK HEALTH

The Essential Guide

KT-194-782

ACC. No. BK55069

CLASS No. 641·563

MID CHESHIRE COLLEGE

ORDER No. m207 8553

Ester Davies

BK55069

First published in Great Britain in 2008 by
Need2Know
Remus House
Coltsfoot Drive
Peterborough
PE2 9BF
Telephone 01733 898103
Fax 01733 313524
www.need2knowbooks.co.uk

All Rights Reserved
© Ester Davies 2008
SB ISBN 978-1-86144-061-7
Cover photograph: Paul Bradbury, Getty Images
Author photograph: Julie Ratcliffe Public Relations
Cartoons: Mark Bayliss

Contents

Recipes

Lunches

Cooking Tea the Low Fat Way

Puddings

Entertaining

Introduction

The healthy eating hype

Healthy eating isn't something new; the message seems to have been around for years in magazines and newspapers, on television and radio and even on food packaging. It seems that wherever you turn there is a barrage of information about food; what to eat, what not to eat and foods that have special properties to cure and heal the body. Messages about food are often confusing and contradictory, implying that if you eat this or that you will live longer and improve your mental ability. Some information is true and some isn't, and it is often very difficult to discriminate without knowing the facts.

While there are so many varying views on nutrition - what's good for you and what isn't - the principles of healthy eating are basic and do improve the body's health and self-esteem. Ongoing scientific research has already identified the link between food and wellbeing, but when you're a student leading a busy life on a budget, these two facts can become neglected.

Eating a balanced and varied diet will help you to not only cope and perform better with your course demands, but with the many changes that come with living for the first time as an independent person making your own choices and decisions.

The next few chapters will help to demystify healthy eating for you when time and budget are paramount. You don't want to spend hours in the kitchen but you do want food that makes you feel and look good. By focusing on eating habits and patterns, shopping, food storage, preparation and cooking methods, you will find that it is possible to switch to a healthier lifestyle.

Whether you're already a university student, are leaving home for the first time or just want to learn about healthy eating, this essential guide will equip you with everything you need for a healthier lifestyle. The student diet doesn't have to be just takeaways and microwave meals!

Chapter One

The Basic Student Kitchen Kit

Well, this is it! You've finally moved into digs and you're now faced with setting up your kitchen kit alone.

Chances are that you've never had to plan and organise these things, so before we take a look at healthy eating, you need to get to grips with the basics.

If you've already lived away from home, you've probably already stocked up on a few essential items from your parents, but for the majority of students it's a case of starting from scratch. Very few student kitchens are fully equipped so you'll need to take some items with you.

A good place to start if you haven't got anything is to ask politely for donations from family and friends. Lurking in almost every family kitchen are hordes of utensils and equipment cluttering drawers and cupboards, so there's a good chance you'll get some freebies somewhere along the way. Other useful places to consider are charity shops, car boots, table sales and cheaper bargain shops such as TK Maxx, Super Buys and Woolworths who often have utensils at rock bottom prices. This keeps the cost down radically and gives you more money to spend on other items.

If you want special equipment such as a sandwich maker, toaster, roasting pan with lid or blender, then it might be an idea to put together a list so that your family can buy these items as a birthday present or as a going away gift.

If you're in your second year and are moving into a shared house/flat with your friends, it might be worth planning between you what to take. That way you won't end up with four of everything!

'If you're in your second year and are moving into a shared house/flat with your friends, it might be worth planning between you what to take. That way you won't end up with four of everything!'

Equipment essentials

Cooking healthy food doesn't require any specialised equipment, but non-stick pans can help significantly in reducing the amount of fat you need to add to your cooking.

Here is a basic list of equipment essentials:

Can opener – some cans don't have ring pulls.

Cork screw and bottle opener

2 wooden spoons

1 small knife – for cleaning/peeling vegetables.

1 big knife – for chopping.

Set of measuring spoons – a teaspoon (5ml) and tablespoon (15ml) will be used the most.

Non-stick fish slice or spatula – doesn't scratch your pans and handy to lift food out of the frying pan. This is ideal to use for stir-frying.

Large metal sieve (strainer) – this can double up as a colander for straining pasta.

Medium sized saucepan – good for reheating soups and making curries.

Large non-stick frying pan – good for all sorts of dishes.

Non-stick wok – a very versatile cooking pan that can be used for virtually anything including boiling pasta and rice, Bolognese sauce, soups and, of course, stir-frying.

Square grater – useful as you can grate directly into a container or dish without making any mess.

Potato masher

Potato peeler

Baking tray – for any type of baking or roasting vegetables.

Roasting tin with a lid – this is not only good for roasts but for slow cooking as well.

2 plastic chopping boards – one for raw meat and another for vegetables and fruit. They're easy to keep clean and don't breed bacteria.

2 mixing bowls – one large and one small.

Kettle – this should be provided in the student kitchen at university, so you might want to delay buying this until you've moved in or check with the accommodation office.

Toaster – grills take a long time to heat up and cook. These are super quick and efficient. Again, your student kitchen should come with this, but if you're moving into a house, you'll need to take one with you!

Baking/parchment paper – not to be confused with greaseproof paper as it's silicon coated, which means food doesn't stick to it. The main plus point about this is that you use less fat when roasting meat or vegetables and you don't have to scrub the tin!

Other essentials

Cutlery, dinner plates, bowls, mugs and glasses – it doesn't matter if these don't all match so long as they do the job. Remember that you'll be sharing a kitchen with other students, so don't take the best china as things will get broken and lost!

Cleaning gear – three tea towels, scourer, dishcloths, washing up liquid, pot holder and spray cleaner.

Finally, don't forget sandwich bags, cling-film and aluminium foil.

Don't worry if you forget some of these items – your student union shop should stock the basics, but it's less stressful to get organised beforehand.

Two star cooks

More experienced cooks might want to include the following to their list of items: steamer, blender, garlic crusher, casserole dish and pepper grinder.

The essential store cupboard

Many students' kitchens tend to be small and the chances are that you'll only have a limited amount of store cupboard space for ingredients. If you've checked out your digs already, consider buying a few of the basics before the beginning of term. Many of the ingredients listed below are inexpensive and some will last even up to a year.

If you store similar items of food together, such as canned baked beans, sweetcorn and tuna, this makes it far easier for shopping as you can see fairly quickly whether stocks are low or not.

To keep your stash safe, a padlock and key could be useful on your cupboard so that you know everything is available at any given time, i.e. between lectures, tutorials and afterwards. Student flats/houses are always full of guests wandering around who find themselves tempted by food in cupboards!

What should you take?

Obviously, fresh food will have to be bought when you get to university, but the following items can be taken with you:

- Juice - apple or orange.
- Baked beans – these provide a quick, healthy, easy meal.
- Canned peaches (or any sort of canned fruit) – provide a healthy, easy dessert.
- Canned chickpeas – good for soups and salads.
- Canned kidney beans.
- Canned sweetcorn – can be used in salads, or as jackets potato fillings, etc.
- Coffee and tea.
- Sugar.
- Wholemeal bread.
- Dried fruit – apricots, sultanas, etc.

- Canned whole tomatoes – cheaper than chopped.
- Tomato ketchup.
- Tomato soup – good for sauces.
- Tuna – in brine or spring water.
- Pasta (pasta shells, noodles, spaghetti), brown rice and couscous.
- Cereal – Weetabix and Shreddies.
- Porridge oats – for breakfast and for crumbles.
- Plain flour.
- A jar of pesto - can be used with pasta, as part of a sauce or even as a spread.
- Sunflower oil or light olive oil – unsaturated fats for cooking.
- Non-aerosol cooking spray, e.g. Fry Light olive or sunflower oil.
- Curry paste.
- Salt & pepper.
- Lentils.
- Mustard.
- Oat biscuits - good as healthy snacks.
- Malt vinegar.
- Stock cubes – very good for flavouring dishes.
- Potatoes, onions and garlic - kept in an empty shoe box.
- Herbs and spices – mixed herbs, chicken seasoning, curry powder, chilli powder, cumin, turmeric, coriander and thyme - or any of your favourites!
- All purpose seasoning.
- Semi-skimmed long life milk - useful for emergencies.
- White wine vinegar.
- Soy sauce.
- Worcestershire sauce.

Fridge and freezer foods

Fridge

- Tomato purée.
- Orange/apple juice.
- Low fat spread, e.g. sunflower spread.
- Low fat margarine.
- Fresh lean meat – chicken.
- Eggs.
- Low fat natural yoghurt.
- Low fat cheese.
- Vegetables - tomatoes, peppers carrots, lettuce, etc.

Freezer

- Chicken breasts.
- Frozen vegetables.
- Frozen fruit.
- Bread.
- Oven potato wedges.

Fridge and freezer storage tips

Where to store foods in the fridge

- Always store raw meat (e.g. chicken, fish or seafood) on the bottom shelf of the fridge. Make sure it's kept in the original wrapping or placed in a container or plastic bag to stop any blood or juices dripping onto other foods. This will prevent cross contamination from occurring, so that ultimately you don't get food poisoning.

- Always store any leftover food sensibly in the fridge. Transfer leftovers and food from opened cans into a clean plastic container or a plate covered with cling-film. Not only does this make the food safe but it prevents it from drying out.

- Don't go crazy cramming your fridge with too many foods because this can cause problems with even cold air flow. If this happens, some foods will be different temperatures to others.

- Store milk, fruit juices, margarine, sauces, jars and cheese in the side of the fridge door.

- Keep cooked pies, pizzas and other cooked leftover foods together on the same shelf.

- Yoghurts, soft cheeses, dips and snacky foods should be stored on the top shelf so that you can see them at eye level.

- Store fruit and vegetables in the bottom bins/drawers.

- It's best to store eggs in their container near the top of the fridge, rather than in the side egg compartment of the fridge. This will stop them from getting too warm and having hair line cracks. Fridge doors are opened constantly and the internal temperature of the fridge varies. As a result, eggs can deteriorate very quickly.

Tips on storing foods in the freezer

- Always divide larger cooked portions of food into smaller quantities.

- Make sure the food you want to freeze is wrapped properly and tightly and that the correct container is used.

- Don't cram foods into your freezer and make sure there's space around the frozen foods.

- Check your freezer is at -18°C (0°F) or below so that food is sufficiently frozen.

- Ensure the food you're freezing is in perfect condition before you freeze it.

- Before cooking, always defrost frozen food in either the fridge or in cold water.

Getting to grips with shopping and budgeting

Most students aren't flush with money and are more often than not on a tight budget. However, you needn't worry about eating like a pauper because low cost healthy eating is neither boring nor a drag.

One key aspect to shopping and preparing the week's meals is planning what you're going to cook in advance. Roughly working out the things you're going to make will save time and money.

The first thing you need to do is to work out how much money you can afford to spend each week on food and stick to that amount. If you don't, you'll find yourself on the downhill slippery slope of buying ready meals and takeaways because it's the easy option. However, these foods are probably the most costly and unhealthiest option!

Saving money on food shopping trips

▨ Before you start shopping, always have a list. It's a good idea to have a notepad in your kitchen to make note of any foods you require. Remember, shopping lists are flexible so you can change plans according to special deals that may be available in shops.

▨ Take advantage of specials – there are often good deals in supermarkets e.g. 'Buy one get one free' or 50% extra free. These offers can be a bargain for the essential items you may need, but be careful not to be seduced by food that you don't really want and will never use.

▨ It's a good idea if you can buy in bulk or in larger quantities because this is cheaper in the long run. For food items that you only use occasionally, such as dried herbs and spices, buy only in small quantities. When you're settled in, it might be a good idea to buy some of the larger food items as a group, for example potatoes and onions.

▨ Get into trying the supermarket or corner shop's own brands such as 'value' or 'happy shopper', especially for canned tomatoes, beans, cheese and bread.

▨ Shop in the supermarket at the end of the day, especially on a Sunday when fresh fruit and vegetables near the 'sell by' date are drastically reduced in price.

- If you are able to get to a market you'll find fruit and vegetables much cheaper, but be careful that you don't get persuaded into buying more than you need. Insist on selecting the produce yourself to ensure you're getting quality fruit and vegetables that will keep for much longer.

- Buy seasonal fruit and vegetables because it's far cheaper than anything flown in from abroad.

- If a supermarket is your only option to buy fresh produce then avoid pre-packaged fruit and vegetables. Buying loose amounts is much less expensive.

- Go for frozen vegetables and canned fruit in their natural juices because these are very good alternatives to fresh. They also last longer than fresh fruit and vegetables.

Saving money in the kitchen

- Save on your fuel bills by cooking several meals at the same time by using every bit of space in the oven. (Obviously this is only practical if no one else plans to use the oven for a while!)

- Double up on the quantities of meals that you make. This works out far cheaper and you can freeze the extra meals in the freezer. (It's also useful to have a meal ready in the freezer, for the times you're feeling too tired to cook.)

- Don't be wasteful with fresh fruit and vegetables. Try and plan meals so that fresh fruit and vegetables are used first when they're at their peak, otherwise you'll forget about them in the fridge and will end up throwing them away.

- Don't buy pre-prepared sauces such as pasta and curry sauces. Not only are they expensive but they are often full of fat and additives. Make your own sauces that require fewer ingredients and are easy to prepare. You can add an indulgent touch by adding a teaspoon of pesto to a tomato sauce to give extra added flavour. A jar of pesto could be used in at least six other meals.

- Remember that healthy eating involves basing your meals around starchy foods such as pasta, rice, potatoes, peas, beans and lentils. Not only are starchy foods far better for you but they're also cheaper.

Surviving kitchen mess

Students are notorious for unhygienic kitchen practices – sinks piled up with dirty dishes, overflowing bins and food left on work surfaces. If this sounds like your kitchen, beware. Sooner rather than later illness will strike or, worse still, food poisoning. All of these bad kitchen habits can be avoided by following basic rules in the kitchen, which should be observed by everyone.

Kitchen tips to avoid bugs

- Always wash your hands in the kitchen before and after cooking. This is especially important when handling cooked and raw foods because if you don't, you'll end up spreading bacteria through cross contamination.

- Make sure all work surfaces and the fridge door handle are disinfected with an anti-bacterial cleaner and washed down with a clean, soapy cloth. Use clean tea towels to dry dishes or, if space permits, leave the dishes on the draining board to air dry and then put them away.

- Inevitably, student life is hectic with all its comings and goings and the kitchen can be left in a mess. Try to clean and tidy the kitchen as you go to avoid a big build up of mess. This avoids a big job at the very end or, worse still, facing up to the job when you get back from lectures. At this late stage, cleaning up becomes a daunting, begrudging task you'd rather steer clear of. Messy kitchens can also cause arguments between students!

- Don't ever allow raw and cooked food to come into contact, whether it's in storage or in food preparation. In other words, don't store raw and cooked food together on the same shelf in the fridge. Raw meat should be stored at the bottom of the fridge so that the meat juices don't drip over the other food. When preparing food on a chopping board, don't use the same board for raw and cooked food. You can use a separate board or wipe and turn the board over. Make sure also that the knife is also thoroughly washed in hot, soapy water to stop the spread of bacteria.

- Make sure when you reheat food that it is thoroughly cooked and piping hot. Never reheat any food more than once.

- Don't hold onto any food that has mould growing on it and hope that by cutting it off it'll be okay. Some moulds and fungi are not visible to the human eye but can spread throughout the deteriorated food, producing dangerous food poisoning toxins. So get rid of it!

- 'Use-by' dates are self explanatory. Once the date has passed the food is no longer safe to eat and should be thrown in the bin. 'Best before' usually relates to canned and packaged foods such as pasta or cereal. This means that the food can be eaten a couple of weeks after the date has passed, but it won't taste as good. If the food has the wording 'Eat within 3 days' this means the food should be eaten within this time because E.coli or salmonella will develop after this period, which can result in food poisoning.

- When buying food for freezing ensure it's stored in the freezer as soon as possible. Don't think you're ahead by buying frozen food on the way to lectures where it'll be hanging around for hours thawing on the floor. Never re-freeze food that has defrosted.

- After cooking food, allow it to cool down properly before putting it into the fridge. If food is not properly cooled, bacteria can grow.

Summing Up

- Keep your options open when sorting out your kitchen kit.

- Stick to the basic equipment and build up if you need to.

- Always plan what you're going to buy in advance before you go shopping so you stick to your budget.

- Be a smart shopper and look for special deals, buy fresh vegetables and fruit in season and buy in bulk – this will keep your costs down.

- Follow safe and hygienic food practices and storage in the kitchen to avoid food poisoning - to yourself and your flatmates.

Chapter Two

The Really Useful Cooking Basics

Getting to grips with measuring

Getting your head around measuring isn't difficult. If you've never cooked anything before it's a good idea to use basic measuring tools such as a set of kitchen scales and measuring spoons to make sure you get the right balance of ingredients. You want your recipes to work out, otherwise you can be wasting precious ingredients and time. As a general rule, teaspoons and tablespoons are used when measuring herbs and spices, raising agents and oil.

Ounces and grams are commonly used in recipes. Although an ounce is technically equal to 28.35 grams in cooking, 25 grams is the working equivalent used in the kitchen, which is far easier. Here's a quick guide to getting your head around common measurements in the kitchen.

Two of the most common measurements you're likely to use in the kitchen are;

1 teaspoon or tsp = 5 ml, 1 tablespoon or tbsp = 15ml.

Imperial/metric conversions

Dried weights are measured in pounds (lb) and ounces (oz) or grams (g) and kilograms (kg). Liquids are measured in pints (pt) and fluid ounces (fl oz) or millilitres (ml) and litres (l).

Dried weights	
Ounces (oz)	Grams (g)
1oz	25g
2oz	50g
3oz	75g
4oz	100g
5oz	125g
6oz	150g
7oz	175g
8oz	200g
1lb	450g
2lb	1kg

Liquids	
Pints (pt)	Millilitres (ml)
¼ pt	125ml
½ pt	250ml (¼ litre)
¾ pt	375ml
1	500ml (½ litre)
1 ½ pt	750ml (¾ litre)
2 pt	1000ml (1 litre)

Temperature guide

Oven temperatures can be quite tricky, so here's a quick conversion of degrees Fahrenheit to Centigrade, as well as the gas mark settings which may be useful should you have a gas cooker in your student kitchen.

When a recipe refers to a slow or cool oven temperature this range is between 275°F/140°C to 325°F/170°C. This temperature range is ideal for slow roasting and casseroles. Moderate temperatures which start at 350°F/180°C to 400°F/200°C are suitable for baking cakes and roasting meat. High temperatures ranging from 425°F/220°C to 500°F/250°C are ideal for scones and filo pastry.

Getting your oven to the correct temperature is very important to get the best results. It's also important to know that preheating the oven for at least 10 minutes allows the cooker to reach the correct temperature.

Electric temperature	Gas temperature	Heat
275°F/140°C	Mark 1	COOL
300°F/ 150°C	Mark 2	
325°F/ 170°C	Mark 3	
350°F/ 180°C	Mark 4	MODERATE
375°F/ 190°C	Mark 5	
400°F/ 200°C	Mark 6	
425°F/ 220°C	Mark 7	HOT
450°F/ 230°C	Mark 8	
500°F/ 250°C	Mark 9	

Useful cooking temperatures for meat

Chicken 20 minutes per 450g /1lb + 20 minutes extra

Beef 20 minutes per 450g /1lb + 20 minutes extra

Pork 25 minutes per 450g /1lb + 25 minutes extra

Lamb 25 minutes per 450g /1lb + 25 minutes extra

Getting to grips with cooking jargon

If you're not used to cooking and following recipes you may be unfamiliar with certain jargon that's used. Here's a quick guide to words you might come across in recipes.

Bake - Cooking in the oven (dry heat). You use this method for cakes, biscuits, slices and savoury dishes.

Beat - Mixing ingredients very quickly and introducing air into the mixture using a wooden spoon, fork, electric beater or whisk.

Blend - Mixing together either cornflour or flour with a little cold liquid until you form a paste. This can be added to soups, gravies, stews or stir-fries to thicken them.

Boil - Cooking in a very hot liquid. Rice, pasta and vegetables are all required to reach boiling point.

Chop - Ingredients are placed onto a chopping board and using a cutting action (up and down) with a sharp knife you make the ingredients smaller in size.

Cream - Combining butter or margarine together with sugar and beating it until the mixture resembles whipped cream.

Dough - A thick mixture of uncooked flour and liquid which can sometimes have other ingredients added to it.

Fold - Combining either a whisked or a creamed mixture with other ingredients so that the dish remains light and no air is lost. This is a very gentle action using a large spoon that is moved down the side of the mixture, underneath it and brought up over the top.

Fry - Cooking food in either hot fat or oil.

Grate - Shaving firm foods such as cheese or carrot into smaller shreds.

Grill - Cooking food under direct heat under a grill.

Knead - Working a flour dough with the palm of the hand.

Marinade - A mixture of oil, lemon, wine or soy sauce into which food is placed for a given time. This helps to soften and add flavour to the food.

Mash - A pulverising action that makes a food become smooth.

Poach - Cooking in an open pan using a gentle heat.

Roast - Cooking in a roasting tin in the oven, e.g. meat or vegetables.

Rub in - To put small pieces of butter or margarine into flour, which is rubbed in using the fingertips so that it resembles breadcrumbs.

Sauté - To cook in an open pan over a high heat with oil or butter, stirring or shaking the pan so that it jumps to stop food from sticking to the pan.

Season - To add flavour by adding seasonings to a food, usually salt and pepper.

Sift - To put dry ingredients through a sieve to remove lumps and to add air.

Simmer - To keep a liquid just below boiling point so that the liquid is just moving.

Steam - Food is cooked by steam passing through holes in a pan or in a specially designed steamer.

Whisk - To beat air in rapidly to a mixture.

How to test if it's done?

Hamburgers and meatballs

Don't rely just on the outside being browned. The best test is to cut open the meat and if there is no blood running out or there are no pinkish bits present, it's cooked.

Cakes

Place a sharp pointed knife, or better still a skewer, into the centre of the cake and if it comes out clean it's baked. Another test is to gently touch the centre of the cake while it's in the oven and if it springs back it's baked.

Chicken and other meat

Apart from the calculated time and the extra cooking time that a particular meat requires, you can also tell whether it's cooked if the juices run clear and there are no any pinkish, uncooked bits near the bone. If this isn't the case, the meat is not cooked and will need extra cooking time (see page 23).

Pasta

The cooking time for different types of pasta varies on whether it's fresh, pre-cooked or dried. Cooked pasta swells around the edges and expands slightly. Using a fork to bite through the centre will tell you if it's 'al dente' (just tender to the bite) or not. The pasta should be chewy but not starchy.

Rice

Rice grains swell in size when they're cooked. To test whether your rice is cooked, bite into a grain. If it's starchy, it's not ready.

Do sausages need to be pricked?

Don't prick sausages before cooking them as this will result in a loss of moisture and flavour, and never grill or fry them on a high heat as this causes them to burst open. By cooking them over a moderate heat they retain their shape and flavour.

How to test whether an egg is fresh or not

Place the egg in a bowl of salted water. If the egg sinks, it's fresh. If it floats (the air sac in the egg has got bigger because it has deteriorated) get rid of it because it's off and can't be used.

The big don'ts in the kitchen

- Never go shopping when you're hungry. Make sure you have something to eat beforehand or you'll spend a lot more money on food!

- If you're in a hurry and can't wash up always make sure you soak dishes and pans in hot water and detergent. This makes them easier to clean later on, with no need to scrub!

- Never reheat cooked rice more than once. Rice is very prone to food poisoning bacteria and can make you very ill.

- Always make sure pork is thoroughly cooked and not pinkish on the inside.

- Many of the chickens you buy contain the salmonella bacteria. Always make sure chicken is thoroughly cooked; clear running juices and no pinkish colour around the bone tell you that it's ready.

- Never eat raw or undercooked kidney beans. They contain a toxic agent called lectin which can cause botulism. Make sure you soak and cook raw kidney beans properly otherwise they can cause nausea and diarrhoea. In the worst cases, they can result in death from the paralysis of the lungs.

Getting confident with the cooking basics

Cooking and preparing healthy, low fat food involves using different cooking methods which retain the nutrition in the food. Cooking methods such as steaming, grilling, boiling and microwaving are all good for creating delicious tasting food. Other healthy methods include using non-stick pans with unsaturated spray or oil.

Jacket potatoes

These are high in vitamin C and fibre (found in the skin). They can be prepared in several different ways: baked in the oven, cooked in the microwave or partly cooked in the microwave and then finished off in the oven.

'Never go shopping when you're hungry. Make sure you have something to eat beforehand or you'll spend a lot more money on food!'

Baked in the oven
1. Preheat the oven to 180°C/350°F/Gas Mark 4.
2. Wash the potato under cold water and pierce several times with a knife.
3. Place in the oven and bake for approximately 1 hour. More time may be needed depending on the size of the potato.

Cooked in the microwave
1. Wash and pierce as above.
2. Place into the microwave for 4 - 5 minutes (this depends on the wattage of the microwave) until cooked.
3. Once cooked, allow to stand for several minutes (the inside of the potato is still cooking).

As a student with limited time, this will probably be the more popular method!

Part microwave/part oven
1. Wash and pierce as above.
2. Place into the microwave for 3 minutes until partly cooked.
3. Transfer to the oven set at 200°C/400°F/Gas Mark 6 for a further 25 - 30 minutes until the potato is baked and looks crisp.

Potato wedges

Once again, these are high in vitamin C and fibre (found in the skin). So you don't lose too much vitamin C these need to be coarsely cut. You can add many different sorts of seasonings to make them more interesting: thyme, rosemary, garlic, coarse rock salt, pepper and Cajun spices are just a few ideas.

Baked in the oven
1. Preheat the oven to 200°C/400°F/Gas Mark 6.
2. Wash and scrub the potatoes under cold water.
3. Cut the potatoes in half lengthways and then into chunks.
4. Using a sandwich/freezer bag, add the seasonings and a tablespoon of sunflower or olive oil.
5. Place the chunks of potato into the bag, close and shake so that each piece is covered.
6. Turn out onto a baking tray and place into the oven for 45 minutes or until crisp.

Boiled potatoes

These can be very nutritious provided they are cut into chunks and the water just covers the potatoes. The same applies to new potatoes but all you need with these is to scrub them, leaving the skin on, and place them into enough water to cover them. If you add too much water, all the vitamin C (water soluble) content seeps into the water and you don't benefit from getting all that goodness.

Boiled on the hob
1. Wash the potatoes and peel the skin.
2. Cut into large chunks, place into a saucepan and just cover with cold water. Add a pinch of salt.
3. Bring to the boil with a lid on the pan.
4. Once the water reaches the boil, reduce the temperature to a simmer.
5. Cook for 25 minutes until the potatoes have softened.
6. After the potatoes are cooked, drain the water off and serve.

Roast potatoes

These can be very nutritious, provided they are cut into larger pieces as this retains the vitamin C content. By adding only a small amount of unsaturated (sunflower or olive oil) fat to them this is still tasty and considered to be a healthy option.

1. Preheat the oven to 200°C/400°F/Gas Mark 6.
2. Peel the potatoes and cut into chunks. Place in a pan of boiling water and cook for 3 - 4 minutes to start the softening process.
3. Drain the potatoes and give them a shake in the sieve to roughen the surface. This gives a fluffy texture when they are cooked.
4. Place 2 tablespoons of oil on a baking tray and put in the oven until the oil is hot.
5. Add the potatoes to the baking tray and cook for 45 minutes to an hour, until golden.

Rosemary & Thyme Roast Potatoes

Serves 2

Nutrition	per serving
Calories (kcal)	245.7
Carbohydrate (g)	45.8
Protein (g)	5.4
Fat (g)	5.2
Fibre (g)	4.2

Ingredients
2 baking potatoes, cut into similar sized chunks
½ tsp dried rosemary
1 tsp dried thyme
1 clove garlic, peeled and crushed
2 tsp sunflower/olive oil
Salt and pepper (pinch)

Method
1. Preheat the oven to 200°C/400°F/Gas Mark 6.
2. Peel and cut the potatoes into chunks and place into a freezer/sandwich bag.
3. Add the rosemary, thyme, crushed garlic, oil, salt and pepper.
4. Close the bag and shake well until the potatoes are covered with the oil and seasonings.
5. Place onto a baking tray and put into the oven for 45 minutes or until the potatoes are crisp.

Spicy Potato Wedges

Serves 2

Nutrition	per serving
Calories (kcal)	271.0
Carbohydrate (g)	46.5
Protein (g)	5.6
Fat (g)	7.6
Fibre (g)	4.5

Ingredients
2 baking potatoes with skin on, cut into 8 pieces
1 tsp all purpose seasoning
½ tsp of cracked black pepper
1 tbsp sunflower/olive oil

Method
1. Preheat the oven to 220°C/425°C/Gas Mark 7.
2. Combine the seasoning, pepper and sunflower oil together in a sandwich/ freezer bag.
3. Place the potato wedges into the bag, squeeze the bag tightly and shake vigorously until the seasoning coats each potato wedge.
4. Place onto a baking tray and cook for 30 - 35 minutes until brown and crisp.

Vegetable Serving Size	Vitamins and Minerals	How to prepare it	Boiling
Green Beans 75g/3oz per person	Vitamin C and fibre.	Top and tail the bean at each end.	Boil water in a saucepan with a little salt over a high heat. Boil green beans for 3 - 4 mins until tender and crisp.
Broccoli 2 florets per person	Vitamins A, B2, C, iron, fibre and potassium.	Wash and cut the head into florets.	Boil broccoli in salted water for 4 - 7 mins until tender and crisp.
Carrots 1 medium size per person	Vitamins A, C, potassium and fibre.	Peel or scrub peel. Slice or cut into sticks.	Boil in salted water for 3 mins until crisp and tender.
Cauliflower 2 florets per person	Vitamin C.	Cut off florets from the stalk into pieces.	Boil in salted water for 6 mins until tender.
Cabbage & Greens ¼ head or 50g per person	Vitamins A, B6, C, folic acid and potassium.	Remove outer leaves. Keep greens whole and shred cabbage.	Boil cabbage or greens in salted water for 3 - 5 mins until just tender.
Leeks 1 medium size per person	Vitamins A, B6, C, E, iron, potassium and fibre.	Cut off the stem and green leaves. Cut in half to wash out soil and cut into slices.	Prepare leeks and boil in salted water for 12 – 15 mins.
Corn on the cob 1 cob per person	Vitamin C, folic acid, thiamin and potassium.	Cut off husk and silk from ear of the corn.	Boil corn cob in salted water for 30 mins.

Steaming	Microwaving	Stir-fry
Fill pan with a third of water and place steamer on top. Bring to the boil and add beans. Steam for 2 - 3 mins.	Place in micro dish with 1 tbsp water. Cook for 3 - 4 mins on HIGH. Take out and stir and stand for 3 mins.	Heat up a little oil in a wok or pan and stir-fry for 3 - 4 mins until the skin gets slightly wrinkly.
Place into steamer once water has heated up. Steam for 3 - 5 mins.	Place in a micro dish with 1 tbsp water. Micro on HIGH for 3 - 5 mins and stand for 1 min.	Heat a little oil in a wok or pan and stir-fry broccoli for 3 - 5 mins.
Place carrots into steamer once water has heated up and steam for 2 minutes.	Place in micro dish and cover sliced carrots. Cook for 3 mins on HIGH. Take out and stand for 2 mins.	Heat a little oil in a wok or pan and stir-fry for 4 mins until crisp.
Place cauliflower florets in steamer once the water has heated up. Steam for 5 mins.	Place into micro dish and add 1 tbsp water. Cover and cook for 1 min. Stand for 1 min.	Heat up oil in a wok or pan and stir-fry cauliflower for 4 mins.
Place into steamer once water has heated up and steam for 2 - 3 mins.	Place in micro dish with 1 tbsp water. Cook on HIGH for 2 mins.	Heat up a little oil in a pan or wok and stir-fry greens for 2 mins and finely shredded cabbage for an extra minute.
Place into steamer once the water has heated up. Steam for 3 - 4 mins.	Cut leek in 2 - 3 places. Add 2 tbsp water in a micro dish and cook for 3 mins on HIGH. Take out and stand for 3 mins.	Heat up oil in a wok or pan, add leeks and stir-fry for 2 mins.
Place into steamer once water has boiled. Steam for 15 - 20 mins.	Wrap in cling-film or place in a micro dish with 4 tbsp water. Cook for 3 - 4 minutes. Take out and leave to stand for 3 - 5 minutes.	Not suitable to stir-fry whole.

Vegetables

It's important to stress that vegetables can be prepared in several low fat cooking methods: boiling, microwaving, steaming or stir-frying in a non-stick wok/pan with very little fat. The best two methods are steaming and microwaving as these tend to keep in the nutritional value, provided you don't extend the cooking time.

Root vegetables such as swede and carrots tend to take longer to cook than green vegetables such as spinach, broccoli and beans. The yellow vegetables contain vitamin A (fat soluble) and they are more resistant to heat, but to retain their nutrition they should not be over cooked.

The table on the previous pages shows you how popular vegetables can be prepared and cooked using a low fat cooking method.

'All pasta contains B vitamins and some minerals, but whole wheat pasta is far better nutritionally as it provides fibre, vitamins and minerals.'

Pasta

Pasta comes in all different shapes and sizes – spaghetti, noodles, fettucine, shells, spirals and lasagne sheets, to name a few. All pasta contains B vitamins and some minerals, but whole wheat pasta is far better nutritionally as it provides fibre, vitamins and minerals.

Fundamentally all pasta needs to be cooked, but the cooking time varies according to whether it's fresh, dried, pre-cooked or quick cook, white or whole wheat. White pasta cooks far quicker than whole wheat pasta, which requires extra cooking time.

Easy Cooked Pasta

Serves 4

Ingredients
6 x 250ml cups water
125g pasta (dried, not quick cook)
½ tsp salt
1 tsp olive oil

Boiled on the hob
1. Place the oil, salt and water into a large saucepan and bring to the boil with the lid on the saucepan (this speeds up the boiling).
2. Once the water is boiling, add the pasta and stir. Make sure everything is covered in the water.
3. Reduce the heat slightly (don't place the lid on the saucepan) and continue to boil, stirring once or twice so that the pasta separates. Cook for 15 – 20 minutes until al dente (or just tender to the bite).
4. Drain the pasta in a colander or a sieve and serve.

Cooked in the microwave
1. Place the pasta, salt, oil and water together in a large microwave dish and stir. Cover and cook on HIGH for 4 minutes.
2. Open the microwave and stir. Cover and cook on MEDIUM for another 9 minutes.
3. Once al dente, drain the pasta into a colander or sieve.

Easy Tomato Pasta Sauce

Serves 4

Nutrition	per serving
Calories (kcal)	113.1
Carbohydrate (g)	9.3
Protein (g)	2.5
Fat (g)	7.5
Fibre (g)	2.4

Ingredients

2 tbsp olive oil
1 stick celery, sliced thinly
1 clove garlic, peeled and crushed
1 carrot, sliced thinly
1 medium onion, sliced thinly
1 x 400g can tomatoes
3 tbsp tomato purée
1 tsp mixed herbs
150ml water
½ tsp salt
½ tsp pepper

Method

1. Heat the oil in a non-stick pan and add the vegetables. Stir continuously for about 5 minutes or until soft.
2. Add the tomatoes, tomato purée, mixed herbs and water. Mix well.
3. Allow the sauce to simmer for 45 minutes, stirring at intervals. Season with the salt and pepper and serve with pasta.

Rice cooking guide

There is a multitude of different types of rice available on the market. Examples include Basmati, Jasmine, long grain, short grain, wild rice, Arborio rice, brown, American rice and pudding rice. Depending on the type of rice, the cooking time and texture once it's cooked varies.

Rice provides carbohydrates and B vitamins, but brown rice has an added bonus in that it contains fibre and more vitamins and minerals. The wholegrain found in brown pasta gives it a distinctive nutty taste. It takes longer to cook because of the outer bran covering but it retains its shape better when you make stir-fries. Quick cook brown rice is now available in supermarkets and other stores, so give it a try.

'Rice provides carbohydrates and B vitamins, but brown rice has an added bonus in that it contains fibre and more vitamins and minerals.'

Easy Cooked Rice

Serves 4

Ingredients
250g brown rice, washed in a sieve and drained
½ tsp salt
500ml water

Boiled on the hob
1. Place the rice and salt in a small saucepan, add water and stir.
2. Place the lid on the saucepan and bring the water to the boil.
3. Once the water is rapidly boiling, reduce the heat and simmer, take the lid off and continue to cook for 20 - 25 minutes or until the water has been absorbed and the rice is tender.
4. Replace the lid on the saucepan. Turn off the heat and allow the rice to stand for a further 5 minutes. You can then fluff up the rice with a fork and serve.

Cooked in the microwave
1. Place the rice and salt in a microwave dish and pour over boiling water and cover. Ensure you allow some space for the steam to escape to avoid the water from boiling over.
2. Cook on HIGH for 25 minutes, then stand for 5 minutes before fluffing up.

Eggs

Eggs are a good source of high quality protein, iron, phosphorus and vitamins A and D. Quick to prepare and easy to digest, they're an ideal meal at anytime. Eggs can be eaten at breakfast, at lunch time or even as part of an evening meal. They can be prepared several ways including poached, scrambled, dry fried, softly boiled or microwaved. Just as a word of warning though, don't contemplate placing a whole shelled egg into the microwave and cooking it. It is liable to explode and make a massive mess because of the build up of internal pressure. Not only that, but the smell is pretty dire as well!

Poached on the hob
1. Boil 5cm of water in a saucepan. Add 6 drops of vinegar and a pinch of salt.
2. Break the egg into a cup and then gently slide it into the saucepan.
3. Simmer on a low heat for 2 - 3 minutes, until the egg white sets.

Poached in the microwave
1. Break the egg into a microwave dish.
2. Prick the egg white and yolk, and cover loosely with cling-film.
3. Microwave on HIGH for 30 seconds. Take out of the microwave and stand for 20 seconds.

Scrambled on the hob
1. Whisk together the egg, salt, pepper and 1 tablespoon of milk with a fork.
2. Using a low fat cooking spray, squirt 3 shots into a saucepan.
3. Once the pan has heated up, pour in the egg mixture. Stir until it forms soft curds.

Scrambled in the microwave
1. Place ¼ teaspoon of low fat margarine in a microwave bowl and cook on HIGH for 10 seconds.
2. Whisk the egg, 2 tsp milk, salt and pepper together.
3. Pour into a bowl with melted margarine and mix. Microwave on HIGH for 30 seconds. Stir the set egg pieces around from the outside to the centre.
4. Microwave on HIGH for 20 seconds.

Dry fried on the hob

1. Spray the frying pan with low fat spray and heat until the oil disappears.
2. Crack an egg into the frying pan.
3. Cook for 3 minutes until the white has set.
4. Turn over if desired.

Softly boiled on the hob

1. Fill a small saucepan with water halfway up the pan and add a pinch of salt. Bring to the boil.
2. Once a rapid boil is reached, gently lower an egg balanced on a tablespoon into the water. Reduce the heat.
3. Boil for 3 minutes until soft. If you want a hard boiled egg, longer time will be required.

Omelette on the hob

1. Whisk together two eggs, salt and pepper until frothy.
2. Preheat a frying pan with 3 sprays of low fat spray.
3. Pour in the eggs and cook until bubbles appear and the omelette sets. Tilt the pan away from you and loosen the sides.
4. Add any flavourings such as sliced mushrooms or lean ham on one half and then fold the other half over the top.

Omelette on the hob and under the grill

1. Follow steps 1 - 3 in above method.
2. Place the omelette under a hot grill and cook until the surface is set and browned.

Summing Up

- If you're an inexperienced cook, stick to using teaspoons (tsp), tablespoons (tbsp) and other units of measuring when following recipes.

- Become familiar with oven temperatures and keep a chart handy in the kitchen for quick reference.

- Get used to cooking terms and try different cooking techniques.

- Be careful not to prepare raw and cooked foods on the same chopping board.

- Clean as you go to avoid a build up of mess in the kitchen (and arguments with fellow housemates!).

Chapter Three

The Low Down on Healthy Eating

The general view of healthy eating is that it is complex and not easily understood. In fact, healthy eating is not rocket science but, put simply, you need to select a variety of different foods each day to give your body a balance of nutrients. This correct balance enables the body to function effectively.

Nutritionists, dieticians and health professionals use one universal model - The Eat Well Plate. The message is straight forward: you need to eat more starchy cereals, potatoes, cereal products, fruits and vegetables; a smaller amount of meat, eggs, alternatives and dairy products; and a very small amount of fatty and sugary foods.

What's a healthy diet?

Eating a healthy diet involves choosing food from the five food groupings every day and making sure that you eat certain amounts from each. You should aim to eat a variety of different foods and any food that you choose shouldn't make you feel guilty. No food is forbidden!

The type of foods you eat will make you feel better. It's about eating more of the foods that make you feel good, such as starchy cereals, potatoes, fruit and vegetables, and less of the fatty and sugary foods.

Healthy Food Plate

33% Bread, rice, potatoes, pasta and other starchy foods

15% Milk and dairy foods

8% Foods and drinks high in fat and/or sugar

33% Fruit and vegetables

12% Meat, fish, eggs, beans and other non-dairy sources of protein

Percentages used are those recommended by the Food Standards Agency. www.food.gov.uk

Eat more unprocessed starchy cereals

Health professionals are always going on about eating more starchy cereals, potatoes and cereal products each day, suggesting that they should make up the main part of meals. Starchy unprocessed cereals such as wholemeal pasta, rice, bread and oats, and cereal products such as Weetabix, Shreddies and muesli are definitely better than white starchy cereals.

* You should aim to eat three wholegrain or whole wheat cereals a day. These unprocessed cereals make you feel more satisfied and are released into the bloodstream slowly so blood sugar levels are more stable. This means you won't experience the sugar lows and crave sugary foods throughout the day.

* Not only do starchy cereals provide you with energy but they also contain B vitamins and minerals. These are important for the nervous system and will stop you from being irritable.

* The fibre content in unprocessed cereals will keep your appetite satisfied. You won't have the hunger pangs in the middle of lectures and you'll be regular, so no need for any constipation pills or potions!

* Don't be conned into thinking that quick fixes like white bread, rolls and crisps will give you more energy. Of course the processed foods do get into the blood stream quicker but you also lose that energy just as fast. It's actually a quick burst of energy rather than the long haul.

Go large on fruit and vegetables

You need to eat plenty of fruit and vegetables, ideally five in total each day. Fruits and vegetables are loaded with fibre, low in fat and, above all, low in calories! As an added bonus they provide you with protective vitamins and minerals, such as antioxidants which are believed to have a role in fighting some cancers and heart disease. Many fruits and vegetables also contain a high amount of folic acid, vitamin C and potassium; however, natural fruit or vegetable juice (100%) doesn't as the juicing process takes the fibre out.

'You need to eat plenty of fruit and vegetables, ideally five in total each day. Fruits and vegetables are loaded with fibre, low in fat and, above all, low in calories!'

Eating fresh fruits and vegetables are not the only option to you in meeting the five a day target. You can buy chilled, canned, frozen or dried - they're all good provided they don't come in sugared syrups or have sugar added to them. Don't forget that pasta sauces, soups and fruit puddings also count towards your five a day.

Vitamin and mineral goodness

The importance of fruits and vegetables can't be stressed enough, especially in relation to their vital role in the body. Vitamins and minerals are required in very tiny amounts so you don't need too much to get the balance right.

Vitamins are measured in micrograms (mg: a thousand = gram) and minerals are measured in macrograms (mcg: a thousand = microgram) which are even smaller.

As vitamins and minerals are required in such small quantities, the danger of overdosing on individual vitamin and mineral pills is very real and should be avoided. This is especially true with fat soluble vitamins like vitamin A as it can be stored in the liver if in excess and can cause toxicity.

The right mix of fruit and vegetables

A sure fire way of getting the balance right is by eating a combination of five a day to ensure the body's well being. Eating every day a portion serving from each of these main groupings below, ensures the body is getting enough vitamins A, B complex, C, D, E and K. These protect the body from anti-ageing and cancers.

- Dark green leafy vegetables - broccoli, cabbage, sprouts, kale and spring greens are all cruciferous veggies, belonging to the same plant family. These contain vitamins A (beta carotene), C and E which are antioxidants. The phytochemicals in these vegetables help to strengthen the body's immune system.

- Berries and citrus fruits – strawberries, raspberries, blackberries, kiwi, oranges, satsumas and grapefruit all contain vitamin C.

- Yellow and orange vegetables – mango, melon, apricots, peaches, pumpkin squash and carrots all contain vitamin A.

Quick ways to get more fruit and vegetables into your diet

- Add dried, fresh or canned (drained) fruit to breakfast cereals; apricots, peaches, sultanas, sliced banana, strawberries or whatever you fancy.

- Drink a glass fruit juice (apple or orange) with your breakfast cereal. This helps to absorb the iron.

- Try eating a bowl of fruit with some low fat yoghurt and a sprinkling of sunflower or pumpkin seeds.

- Sprinkle dried fruit onto porridge.

- Make up some pancakes or scotch pancakes (you can have the batter in a jug in the fridge prepared in advance) and serve with stewed apples, canned peaches or berries.

- Ready-to-go mixed vegetable strips are great as snacks; carrots, peppers, cucumber – these can be cut up and stored in an airtight container in the fridge.

- Add more vegetables such as peppers, mushrooms, sweetcorn and broccoli (lightly microwaved) to plain pizzas.

- Get into making soup. Soups can be chunky or smooth, it really doesn't matter. Great combinations include carrot and coriander, tomato and basil or potato and leek.

- Don't do dull, boring, lifeless salads. Instead, add roasted vegetables, chickpeas and avocado – be adventurous!

- Add vegetable fillings like homemade low fat coleslaw to jacket potatoes.

What is a portion of fruit and vegetables?

1 portion = any of these

- 3 pieces of dried apricots.

- 2 broccoli florets.

- 1 medium glass of orange juice.

- 1 apple.

- 3 tablespoons of canned kidney beans, drained.
- 3 tablespoons of sweetcorn kernels.
- 1 handful of grapes.
- 1 medium banana.
- 2 tablespoons of baked beans.
- 7 strawberries.
- 2 canned peach halves.
- 3 tablespoons of peas.
- 1 cereal bowl of mixed salad.
- 7 cherry tomatoes.
- 1 medium pear.
- 2 satsumas.
- 1 tablespoon of raisins.
- 2 medium plums.
- 12 canned pineapple chunks.
- 1 handful of vegetable sticks (peppers and carrots).

'By avoiding too much red meat, you can prevent the risk of heart disease in the future.'

Go easy on meat, eggs, alternatives and dairy products

You don't need large amounts of meat and alternatives, and even a lower amount for dairy foods. Only a little (36g - 55g, depending on your sex and weight, which is 15% of your daily calories) amount of protein is required per day for growth and repair of tissues, which isn't a lot.

By avoiding too much red meat, you can prevent the risk of heart disease in the future. Ideally choose lean meats, such as chicken and turkey, fish and any kinds of beans. All of these foods provide protein, B vitamins and useful minerals such as zinc and phosphorus. Beans and lentils belong to this group and also provide fibre.

Watch out for full-fat dairy foods, meat with fatty bits and chicken with skin on it. Too many nuts and cheese are high in fat, but they do contain some vitamins (A, D and E) and minerals (zinc, iron, calcium and magnesium), so it's not all bad news!

Veggie protein watch

If you're a vegetarian you need to get the balance of proteins right because only foods from an animal source are complete proteins. In other words, they all have the right number of amino acids that the body needs. However, by combining plant foods lacking in certain amino acids, you'll get a complete protein; for example, cereals, nuts and seeds can be combined with legumes (peas and beans). It's also a good idea to drink a glass of fruit juice so that the iron from the plant protein is easily absorbed into the body.

Vegetarian complete protein combos

Bread & peanut butter = complete protein

Rice & beans/peas = complete protein

Corn & milk/cheese = complete protein

Vegetables & lentils/legumes = complete protein

Curb the fatty and sugary foods

Eat other foods like cakes, biscuits, sweets, chocolate, pastry, spreads, butter, margarine, crisps, pies, jam and puddings occasionally. They are usually high in fat or sugar, or both in most cases. Remember that a 'sweet tooth' is usually a 'fat tooth' too.

These foods have very little to offer nutritionally, if at all. If you're an addict and must have them every day, just eat a small amount to satisfy the need.

The good, the bad and the downright ugly fats

There's a lot of confusion about what a good fat is and isn't. All fats except the ugly kind contain essential vitamins A and D. They also have the same calorie value, so a tablespoon of butter has a similar calorie value as a tablespoon of olive oil. The difference between the two is the effects each one has on the body. Eating too much saturated fat (bad) can start to build up on the artery walls, which over time can cause them to block up, making it harder for the body to pump blood through the veins. Unsaturated fat, however, doesn't have this effect on the body.

Here's the low down on fat and what to watch out for:

- **The GOOD: Unsaturated fats**. These come mainly from a plant source and are usually liquid in form at room temperature. Examples include olive oil, sunflower oil, peanut oil, vegetable oil, rapeseed oil, soya oil, corn oil and sesame oil. Other good oils are found in oily fish such as mackerel and sardines (Omega 3) and from nuts and seeds (Omega 6).

- **The BAD: Saturated fats**. These are derived from animals and are solid in form when cooled down. Examples include butter, cheese, dripping, lard, suet, goose fat, the fat around steak and chops, chicken skin and the fat in full-fat milk and cheese.

- **The UGLY: Trans fats.** These fats start out as vegetable oils but go through a chemical process called hydrogenation which changes them into trans fatty acids. When the body breaks these down they are treated in the same way as saturated fats. Trans fats are used extensively in commercially prepared foods. Examples include spreadable margarine, reduced fat spread, packet biscuits, cakes, takeaways, ready meals and fast food.

Fat contents in popular foods

To work out quickly just how much fat is in these foods, work on the basis that a tablespoon equals 15 grams and a teaspoon is equal to 5 grams.

Food	Amount of fat
¼ lb burger	20g
2 large sausages	21g
2 low fat sausages	11g
85g mince with fat	14g
85g mince fat, drained	6g
85g roast chicken, skin on	12g
85g chicken, skin removed	4g
60g streaky bacon, fried	25g
60g streaky bacon, grilled	20g
85g cod in batter	9g
85g cod, steamed	1g
140g thin cut chips	3 tsp
60g cheddar cheese	1 ½ tbsp
60g half-fat cheddar cheese	9g
60g cottage cheese	2g
30g double cream	3 tsp
30g single cream	Heaped tsp
30g low fat yoghurt	0.3g

Fat contents of popular foods per serving

Food	Teaspoons of fat	Amount of fat
Full-fat cheddar cheese (30g)	✓✓✓✓✓	5 tsp fat
Light/half-fat cheddar cheese (30g)	✓✓	1 ½ tsp fat
Skimmed milk (per 250ml glass)		0 fat
Semi-skimmed milk	✓✓	1 ½ tsp fat
Full-fat milk	✓✓✓	3 tsp fat
30g crisps	✓✓✓✓✓✓	6 ¼ tsp fat
30g Pretzels	✓	½ tsp fat
30g cashew nuts	✓✓✓✓✓✓✓✓✓✓✓✓✓	13 tsp fat
Mashed potato (1 scoop)	✓✓	2 tsp fat
Baked or boiled potato		0 fat
Fries (1 portion)	✓✓✓✓✓✓✓✓	8 tsp fat
Luncheon meat (28g)	✓✓✓	2 ½ tsp fat
Tuna (28g)	✓	½ tsp fat
Ham (28g)	✓	1 tsp fat

Simple ways to cut down on fat

- Go easy on spreading butter or margarine onto bread. Just scrape a little over rolls or toast!
- Cut off any visible fat around chops and steak.
- Remove the skin from chicken breasts.
- Use a non-aerosol spray to control the amount of fat added to the frying pan.
- Use baking/parchment paper instead of greasing baking trays or dishes.

Other things to watch out for...

Sugar contents in popular foods

Food	Grams of sugar (per 100 grams)	Teaspoons of sugar	% of total allotted sugar (10 grams)
Doughnut	70	16	700%
Tomato ketchup	36	7	360%
Coca Cola	54	13	540%
Chocolate	29	6	290%
Cake	31	6	310%
Puddings	25	5	250%
Strawberry jam	34	7	340%
Food	**Cubes of sugar**		
Weetabix			
NutriGrain			
Coco Pops			
Coca Cola			
Diet Coke			

Calm down on salt

It's a good idea to be aware of the amount of salt you're eating and avoid salty foods and salt added to food. Be aware of the 'hidden' salt in processed foods such as pastes, sauces, cooked meats, ready meals and takeaways.

Check out the food labels as these will give you more information. While you might not be thinking at all about the effects of too much salt in the long term, it does encourage high blood pressure and increases the risk of heart disease, kidney disease and strokes. Getting into good salt habits will pay dividends in the end.

We only need 6 grams or just over a small teaspoon of salt a day, which isn't much. This amount includes the salt added to food and the foods we eat that have salt in them.

Salt contents in popular foods

Food	Grams of salt (per 100 grams)	% of day's salt (6 grams) total
Pizza	2.2	36.67
Chips	2.3	38.33
Bacon	1.6	26.67
Curry	1.5	25
Pies	1.3	21.67
Fish cakes	1.7	28.33
Bread	1.0	16.67
Pork	1.9	31.67

Need2Know

Take it easy with alcohol

It would be virtually impossible for students to avoid alcohol as it's part of the student social scene. However, you need to be aware that alcohol should never be a substitute for food as it offers very little nutritionally and it's high in calories. In fact, alcohol is almost as high as fat per gram (7 kcal/per gram alcohol compared to 9 kcal/per gram fat).

Eating any fatty and sugary foods and drinking alcohol, even in modest amounts, can stack on the pounds. Fatty kebabs and late night kormas combined with alcohol are a fatty blow out. Not only is there weight gain if taken to excess, but the fat cells in the body increase and it is difficult for these to shrink in size without a lot of dietary changes and exercise.

The key to alcohol is to go easy and stick to the drinking guidelines: 21 units for men and 14 units for women per week. (Source: Department of Health.)

However, it's not all doom and gloom on the alcohol front. In fact, 85ml of wine can raise the level of protective substances called HDL's (high-density lipoproteins) which can remove cholesterol from the blood stream. The good news is that arteries don't get as clogged up with fatty scaling on the walls. If red wine is your thing, then a small amount of it appears to reduce the stickiness of blood platelets, which prevents blood clots. Remember though, the key word is moderation and you can avoid overdoing it with a few simple pointers.

'The key to alcohol is to go easy and stick to the drinking guidelines: 21 units for men and 14 units for women per week.'

Department of Health.

Tips on managing alcohol

- Try and sip your drink slowly. Put your glass down rather than holding it because this will slow down your drinking.

- Alternate alcoholic drinks with soda or mineral water.

- Have two alcohol free days a week.

- Don't mix your drinks.

- Remember to stick to your limit.

- Don't get into drinking rounds; it's expensive and you drink far more.

Pump up the water

Drinking water is always underestimated. The more water you drink, the more you'll feel full and the less you'll snack. The added bonus is that your skin and digestive system will also improve dramatically.

Students are often unaware that they are dehydrated and need water to keep them going through long and gruelling lectures and practical sessions. The lack of water manifests itself in the form of headaches and the inability to concentrate properly. You should aim to drink about eight large glasses (250ml/½ pint) a day, which isn't too difficult to do. Liquid in any form is good, except sugary versions.

You can also include herbal teas and diluted fruit juices. Some fruits and vegetables, such as watermelon, lettuce, cucumber and carrots, also contain a lot of water, which can help you feel re-hydrated. Liquids in the form of tea and coffee don't count because they act as a diuretic and stress the kidneys out. As a result, you'll need to go to the toilet more!

Basically, you really need to drink the pure, unadulterated clear stuff and keep tea and coffee to a minimum. Limit yourself to three cups a day if you can and get into the habit of taking a bottle of water to lectures and seminars.

Recipes packed with fruit and vegetables

Fruit & Seed Salad

Serves 1

Nutrition	per serving
Calories (kcal)	308.6
Carbohydrate (g)	58.3
Protein (g)	6.6
Fat (g)	6.9
Fibre (g)	10.9

Ingredients
1 apple, cut into wedges
1 kiwi, peeled and sliced
1 satsuma/clementine, segmented
1 banana, sliced
2 tbsp low fat natural yoghurt
1 tbsp sunflower seeds

Method
1. Prepare all the fruit and place into a bowl.
2. Add 2 tablespoons of low fat yoghurt.
3. Sprinkle sunflower seeds on top and serve immediately.

Mediterranean Salad

Serves 2

Nutrition	per serving
Calories (kcal)	319.4
Carbohydrate (g)	7.8
Protein (g)	4.9
Fat (g)	29.7
Fibre (g)	2.6

Ingredients
50ml (approx) olive oil
½ tbsp white wine vinegar
Salt and pepper to season (optional)
25g stoned olives
Lettuce, washed and shredded
½ onion, sliced thinly
1 tomato, cut into wedges
½ cucumber, sliced thinly
6 - 8 cubes (1/2 inch size) feta cheese

Method
1. Put the oil, vinegar, salt, pepper and olives into a large serving bowl and mix well.
2. Add the lettuce, onion, tomatoes and cucumber and mix with the dressing.
3. Sprinkle the feta cubes over the top.

Need2Know

Mixed Bean Salad

Serves 4

Nutrition	per serving
Calories (kcal)	181.5
Carbohydrate (g)	19.7
Protein (g)	8.1
Fat (g)	7.9
Fibre (g)	6.2

Ingredients
1 x small can red kidney beans, drained
1 x small can butter beans, drained
½ medium red onion, sliced thinly
80g dwarf green beans, topped and tailed
1 red pepper, seeded and sliced thinly

Dressing
2 tbsp olive oil
1 tbsp white wine vinegar
1 tbsp lemon juice
½ tsp light muscovado sugar
½ tsp chilli sauce

Method
1. Put the canned beans into a large bowl, add the onions and mix together.
2. Cut the green beans in half and cook in boiling water for 8 minutes, until tender. Refresh under cold water and drain again. Add to the mixed beans and onions.
3. Add the pepper to the mix.
4. To make the dressing, place the oil, vinegar, lemon juice, sugar and chilli sauce into a jar/container and shake. Pour the dressing over the salad and mix well.

Vegetable kebabs

8 kebabs

Nutrition	per serving
Calories (kcal)	296.4
Carbohydrate (g)	19.8
Protein (g)	4.3
Fat (g)	22.7
Fibre (g)	3.6

Ingredients
8 bamboo skewers, soaked in water overnight
3 courgettes, cut into thick slices
8 boiled and cooled salad potatoes
2 red peppers, seeded and chopped into even sized chunks
2 green peppers, seeded and chopped into even sized chunks
8 cherry tomatoes
4 medium red onions, cut into quarters
8 button mushrooms

Marinade
12 tbsp sunflower oil
Juice and zest from 1 lime (or bottled juice)
2 tsp of brown sugar
3 tsp mixed herbs
4 tbsp balsamic vinegar
Salt and pepper (pinch)

Method

1. Prepare the vegetables and spread them on a non-metallic dish in a single layer. Mix the marinade ingredients and pour over the vegetables, ensuring each piece is thoroughly coated. Leave to marinate in the fridge for a few hours.
2. Preheat the grill until hot. Remove the vegetables from the fridge and thread onto the soaked bamboo skewers, ensuring each kebab has an even mix of vegetables.
3. Place the kebabs onto the grill rack set at a medium heat. Turn the kebabs regularly and baste with the remaining marinade until the vegetables are softened and evenly coloured.

Potato Salad with Red Pepper

Serves 4

Nutrition	per serving
Calories (kcal)	244.7
Carbohydrate (g)	26.0
Protein (g)	3.1
Fat (g)	15.0
Fibre (g)	3.1

Ingredients
450g potatoes, peeled and diced
1 onion, sliced thinly
1 stick celery, chopped
1 clove garlic, peeled and crushed
2 red peppers, seeded and sliced
1 tsp mixed herbs
4 tbsp olive oil
Juice of 1 lemon
Salt and pepper to season (optional)

Method
1. Boil the potatoes for 5 minutes, until tender.
2. While the potatoes are cooking, mix the onion, celery, garlic, pepper, mixed herbs, oil, lemon juice, salt and pepper in a bowl.
3. Drain the potatoes and add them to the mixture. Mix all the ingredients together and leave to cool.

Vegetable Pasta Stir-Fry

Serves 4

Nutrition	per serving
Calories (kcal)	494.4
Carbohydrate (g)	73.6
Protein (g)	15.4
Fat (g)	13.7
Fibre (g)	11.9

Ingredients
400g dried whole wheat pasta
2 carrots, sliced thinly
2.5cm piece of fresh ginger root, thinly sliced (optional)
1 onion, sliced thinly
1 garlic clove peeled and sliced thinly
3 celery sticks, sliced thinly
1 red pepper, seeded and sliced thinly
1 green pepper, seeded and sliced thinly
100g baby corn cobs (tinned if fresh not available)
3 tbsp vegetable oil

Sauce
1 tsp cornflour
2 tbsp water
3 tbsp soy sauce
3 tbsp dry sherry
1 tsp clear honey

Method

1. Cook the pasta in a large pan of boiling water. Drain, return to pan, cover and keep warm.
2. Cook the carrots and baby corn cobs in boiling water for 2 minutes. Drain, plunge into cold water and drain again. Keep to one side.
3. Heat the oil in a large pan over medium heat. If using ginger, add to the pan and stir-fry for 1 minute. Remove the ginger with a slotted spoon and discard.
4. Add the onion, garlic, celery and peppers to the oil and stir-fry over a medium heat for 2 minutes. Add the carrots and baby corn cobs and stir - fry for a further 2 minutes, then stir in the pasta.
5. Put the cornflour in a bowl and mix with water to produce a smooth paste. Stir in the soy sauce, sherry and honey.
6. Pour the sauce into the pan, stir well and cook for 2 minutes.
7. Serve with noodles or rice.

Summing Up

To get to grips with adopting a healthier eating lifestyle that is realistic, you need to take the following points on board:

- Understand that healthy eating is about balance and variety.

- Eat more unprocessed starchy cereals, pastas and bread.

- Eat five portions of fruit and vegetables a day, including one dark green leafy vegetable, an orange/yellow vegetable and a citrus/berry fruit each day.

- Limit protein portions to between 36g – 55g each day.

- Watch how much fat you eat and control how much is used in cooking.

- Make sure that unsaturated fats such as sunflower and olive oils are used in cooking.

- Cut down on sugary and salty foods.

- Be aware of how much alcohol you drink and know your limits.

- Increase the amount of water you drink.

Chapter Four

The Feel Good Guide

Yin and yang

It has long been known in Asian cultures the value of eating well and balancing the foods you put into your body. In our culture 'super foods' are known, but their potential to cure hasn't yet been explored in a big way. Asian culture takes this a step further by not only eating specific foods to feel better, but cooking certain dishes that can help the body to cope with and overcome stress, colds, coughs and reduced energy levels. Certain foods are also eaten to maintain energy levels and cope with PMS.

Stress, reduced energy levels and illness in the form of colds, viruses and coughs are all common complaints to students. Controlling the food you eat and the way it's cooked will go a long way in making you feel better within yourself and preventing illness at exam time.

Super foods

Here's a list of some super foods you need to get into a habit of eating on a regular basis:

Chilli peppers – good for smokers because they help the lungs and dissolve any blood clots in the body.

Apples – protect your heart, lower blood pressure, help prevent cancer and help you if you want to lose weight.

Spinach – helps to fight against cancer and lowers your cholesterol level.

Beans – helps to lower cholesterol, control insulin levels and boosts your fibre intake.

Broccoli – contains five times more of the cancer busting substance than any other food.

Watercress – very high in vitamin C, A and calcium.

Blueberries – high in vitamin C and can beat bouts of moodiness and help with your memory.

Stress busting

'The key to boosting energy levels is to get more vitamins B and C into your body to produce extra hormones when you need them most.'

Life as a student can be stressful from the word go – leaving home, setting up digs, getting used to a new place and people, coping with a new course, the demands of studying, unpredictable work schedules and long gruelling hours in tutorials and lectures all take their toll. Not to mention the fact that you're also probably working two jobs and coping with the day to day business of everyday chores. You may feel like you've lost control, that you're helpless and completely exhausted by it all.

If your quick fix solution is to drink energy drinks that are caffeine based, then think again! Although these drinks stimulate your energy levels for a short while, in the long term the effects wear off quickly. The key to boosting energy levels is to get more vitamins B and C into your body to produce extra hormones when you need them most. You also need to make changes to the way you handle stress, especially during exam time when you need all the energy you can get.

Here are some quick tips to help exam stress.

Change your lifestyle

Make sure you get a full eight hours sleep and get into the habit of going to bed early and getting up early. If you live in a noisy student flat, buy some earplugs!

Give homeopathic remedies a go

Go into a health store and buy some Arnica 6c to improve your sleep before going to bed.

Control your brainwaves

Make time each day to lie down quietly for 12 minutes with the palms of your hands turned upwards (so that you don't sleep) and breathe slowly. You may want to listen to calming music to get you into a relaxed state.

Get moving

Just a little exercise each day such as walking around the block will help you to feel more tired, allowing you to sleep better and boost energy levels.

Eat smaller meals

If your day allows it, try eating six meals a day so that your blood sugar levels are more stable and your energy levels remain high. This means there won't be dips in energy levels because the brain is receiving a constant supply of glucose to the bloodstream. It also avoids hunger pangs as your body has a regular supply of food. When you are in lectures or practical sessions all day, get organised and take healthy snacks with you.

Up your complex carbohydrates

Don't be fooled by high sugar and fatty snacks. They'll give you a quick fix, but you'll suffer a come-down in several hours time because of the reduced glycogen in the body, which will make you feel tired and lethargic. Complex carbohydrates such as wholemeal bread, whole wheat pasta and brown rice will keep glycogen (stored carbohydrates in the body) levels high. The key is to eat these unprocessed carbohydrates to keep glycogen levels constant.

Exam stress busting eating plan

Here are a few meal suggestions to control exam stress.

Breakfast

- Branflakes with semi-skimmed milk.
- Fresh fruit.
- Wholemeal toast with honey.
- Glass of pure fruit juice or a smoothie.

Lunch

- Pitta bread with salad and tahini or chicken.
- Jacket potato (no fat added) with baked beans, low fat cheese or a small amount of grated cheddar cheese.

Dinner

- Brown rice with vegetable curry.
- Whole wheat pasta with chicken, vegetables and tomatoes.
- Stir-fry vegetables and chicken served with brown rice.

Banana & Honey Stress Buster

Serves 1

Nutrition	per serving
Calories (kcal)	277.5
Carbohydrate (g)	52.8
Protein (g)	14.2
Fat (g)	0.8
Fibre (g)	6.8

Ingredients
1 banana, sliced
150ml fat free fromage frais
1 tsp honey
4 dried apricots, chopped

Method
1. Slice the banana into a bowl.
2. Pour over the fromage frais.
3. Drizzle over the honey and add the chopped apricots.

Banana & Strawberry Smoothie

Serves 1

Nutrition	per serving
Calories (kcal)	185.0
Carbohydrate (g)	26.4
Protein (g)	9.4
Fat (g)	4.5
Fibre (g)	2.6

Ingredients
½ banana, peeled and sliced
250ml semi-skimmed milk/skimmed milk
3 large strawberries

Method
1. Blend all the ingredients in a mixer.
2. Pour into a tall glass.

Instead of strawberries, you can add whatever soft fruit you have to hand that needs using up.

Curried Bean Jackets

Serves 2

Nutrition	per serving
Calories (kcal)	531.5
Carbohydrate (g)	99.1
Protein (g)	16.4
Fat (g)	8.5
Fibre (g)	13.7

Ingredients
2 baking potatoes, washed and scrubbed
2 tsp sunflower oil
1 small onion, chopped finely
1 tbsp curry paste
1 x 400g can baked beans

Method
1. Pierce the potatoes with a fork and place into the oven set at 200°C/400°F/ Gas Mark 6 for an hour until tender. You can also microwave them on HIGH for 5 minutes or until cooked.
2. Heat the oil in a small non-stick saucepan and sauté the onions for 3 - 4 minutes.
3. Add the curry paste and cook for a further minute.
4. Pour in the baked beans and mix well together.
5. Remove the baked potatoes from the oven and cut lengthways.
6. Top with the curried beans and serve immediately.

Veggie Curry

Serves 4

Nutrition	per serving
Calories (kcal)	170.3
Carbohydrate (g)	23.4
Protein (g)	9.2
Fat (g)	4.8
Fibre (g)	6.4

Ingredients
2 tsp sunflower oil
1 tsp cumin
1 tsp chilli powder
1 tsp turmeric
2 tsp coriander
2 tsp ginger, chopped or 1 tsp powdered ginger
1 clove garlic, peeled and crushed
150g canned kidney beans, chopped
75g green beans, chopped
2 carrots, sliced
1 medium sweet potato, sliced
1 small head broccoli, cut into florets
100g cauliflower, cut into florets
1 pepper, seeded and diced
125ml water
150g natural, low fat yoghurt

Method

1. In a large non-stick saucepan or wok, add the oil and heat until hot.
2. Add all the spices, ginger and garlic, and cook for 2 - 3 minutes to develop the flavour.
3. Add all the vegetables and beans, mix and cook for 5 - 8 minutes.
4. Pour in the water, cover and simmer for 10 minutes.
5. Once the liquid has reduced, take the pan off the heat and add yoghurt.
6. Return the pan to the heat and gently heat through. Don't boil it otherwise the yoghurt will curdle.
7. Serve with brown rice.

Chicken & Vegetable Stir-Fry

Serves 4

Nutrition	per serving
Calories (kcal)	175.5
Carbohydrate (g)	7.6
Protein (g)	17.6
Fat (g)	8.4
Fibre (g)	2.0

Ingredients

2 tbsp olive oil
2 skinless chicken breasts, chopped into thin strips
1 tsp curry powder
1 medium onion, sliced thinly
2 carrots, sliced into thin strips
1 red pepper, seeded and sliced into thin strips
½ pack baby corn, halved
4 tbsp chicken stock or water
2 tbsp tomato purée

Method

1. Heat a large non-stick frying pan or wok over a high heat and add the oil. Add the chicken and curry powder and stir-fry for 2 - 3 minutes, until the chicken is cooked through.
2. Add the onion, carrot and pepper and stir-fry for a further 2 minutes. Add the sweetcorn and stir-fry for another 2 minutes.
3. Add the stock and tomato purée and simmer for 1 - 2 minutes. Serve with brown rice.

Need2Know

Improving your mood

Mood busting

Current research shows that if you eat certain foods together your mood can be affected as well as your energy levels. Within certain foods there are substances that affect the brain's chemical messengers. Eating complex carbohydrates with protein rich foods containing tryptophan (an amino acid) produces the feel good hormone serotonin. High levels of serotonin make you feel happier, whereas lower levels have the opposite effect, making you feel depressed, irritable, sleepy and exhausted.

Eat more carbohydrates

Boost your diet by eating jacket potatoes, whole wheat pasta, wholemeal bread and brown rice in conjunction with protein rich foods containing tryptophan (such as chicken, turkey, tofu, fish) and dairy products (such as low fat cheese and yoghurt). Eating these foods together increases your insulin levels, which at the same time increases your blood levels of tryptophan. By the time this reaches the brain it's converted into serotonin, making you feel great!

> **Complex starchy carbohydrate + tryptophan rich protein = HAPPY MOOD**

'Current research shows that if you eat certain foods together your mood can be affected as well as your energy levels.'

Eat proteins rich in tryptophan

Foods that have high amounts of tryptophan include lean meats, such as turkey and chicken, fish, low fat yoghurt and cheese. Soya products such as soya beans and tofu also contain high amounts. If you have two servings of these foods each day you'll feel changes in your mood.

Big up vitamins B6 and C and minerals (zinc and selenium)

Don't forget vitamins also play a crucial role in helping your mood. Zinc, selenium and vitamins B6 and C are especially important.

Vitamin B6 or folic acid is found in broccoli, brussel sprouts, spinach and other dark green, leafy vegetables. Vitamin C or ascorbic acid is found in citrus fruits, such as oranges, lemons and berries. These two vitamins help to release the action of the carbohydrates and proteins in the body. The mineral zinc (found in seafood, fish and Brazil nuts) and selenium (found in sunflower seeds) also help moods.

Follow through with lifestyle changes

Once you've changed your eating habits to combat the blues, a simple exercise regime and some relaxation also helps. Why not join the gym or find out what classes the sport centre offers?

Beating the blues menu plan

Breakfast

- Muesli.
- Wholemeal toast, low fat cheese and marmite.
- Bovi tonic.

Lunch

- Chickpea and brown rice salad.
- Prawn, spinach and rocket salad.
- Pasta bows with pinenuts.

Dinner

- Chilli con carne with brown rice.
- Turkey and vegetable casserole.

Need2Know

Recipes

Chickpea & Rice Salad

Serves 2

Nutrition	per serving
Calories (kcal)	279.2
Carbohydrate (g)	39.2
Protein (g)	11.2
Fat (g)	8.9
Fibre (g)	7.0

Ingredients
1x 215g can chickpeas, drained
½ cucumber, diced
2 small tomatoes, diced
2 spring onions, sliced thinly
125g cooked brown rice
1 tbsp mint, chopped (optional)
1 tbsp lemon juice
2 tsp olive/sunflower oil
Pepper (to taste)

Method
1. Combine all the prepared ingredients into a bowl and mix together and chill for 30 minutes.

Turkey & Vegetable Casserole

Serves 2

Nutrition	per serving
Calories (kcal)	404.6
Carbohydrate (g)	37.5
Protein (g)	34.8
Fat (g)	13.2
Fibre (g)	5.1

Ingredients
250g turkey, cut into pieces
1 medium onion, sliced thinly
1 green pepper, seeded and diced
1 carrot, sliced
1 tsp mustard
2 tbsp vinegar
¼ tsp thyme or mixed herbs
1 small can of tomato soup

Method
1. Preheat the oven to 180°C/350°F/Gas Mark 4.
2. Arrange the turkey, onion, pepper and carrot in an ovenproof casserole dish.
3. In a bowl, mix together the mustard, vinegar and thyme/mixed herbs with the tomato soup.
4. Pour the tomato mixture over the turkey and vegetables, and place the lid on the dish.
5. Place into the oven for 1 – 1 ¼ hours.
6. Remove from the oven and serve.

Need2Know

Chilli Con Carne

Serves 4

Nutrition	per serving
Calories (kcal)	238.9
Carbohydrate (g)	16.8
Protein (g)	20.4
Fat (g)	10.3
Fibre (g)	4.6

Ingredients
1 tbsp sunflower/olive oil
1 medium onion, sliced thinly
2 cloves garlic, peeled and crushed
250g lean mince beef
½ tsp chilli powder
¼ tsp cinnamon
2 tbsp tomato purée
1 x 200g can kidney beans drained and washed in a sieve
1x 400g can chopped tomatoes
125ml beef stock (125ml mixed with 1 tbsp of soy sauce)

Method
1. Heat the oil in a non-stick wok or large saucepan, add the onions and fry for 6 - 8 minutes until softened.
2. Add the garlic and fry for a further 2 minutes.
3. Add the mince and cook for 10 minutes until browned.
4. Add the chilli powder and cinnamon and cook for 2 - 3 minutes, so that the flavour can develop.
5. Add the tomato purée, mix well and cook for a further 3 minutes.
6. Toss in the kidney beans and mix. Add the tomatoes and beef stock.
7. Bring to the boil and simmer for 25 - 30 minutes. Serve with rice.

Fighting a cold, cough and virus

Invariably at some point you will suffer the dreaded cold, cough or virus. You're more likely to catch a cold or virus when your body is run down and your immune system is low. This usually hits the nose and throat areas and causes them to swell. The mucous membranes in these areas become inflamed and an infection can set in forming inflamation.

If you feel yourself getting run down here are a few suggestions to get you back on the road to recovery.

Keep away from carbohydrates and dairy foods

Avoid eating carbohydrates and dairy foods such as milk, yoghurt and cheese. These foods only make your cold worse by creating excess mucous.

Pump up vitamins C and B and zinc

Eat lots of fresh fruit containing vitamin C, for example berries and citrus fruit. Follow on for two days eating salad, steamed or microwaved vegetables and then eat casserole dishes packed with vegetables. Before you know it, your immune system will be fighting fit again.

Up the garlic and onions

Adding loads of garlic and onions to your cooked dishes helps to breakdown the mucous. Also, if you have a dry and tickly cough, try mixing chopped onion with a bit of honey and eating it a couple of times a day. This will get rid of the mucous from your chest.

Drink loads of fluids

Make sure you keep warm and avoid chilly spots. Drink plenty of warm fluids (but not the alcoholic kind) to get rid of any mucous build up in your body.

Herbal green teas and natural infusions such as lemon grass in warm water are all very good.

Dealing with a fever

Fevers have the exact opposite effect to colds. Usually there is a loss of appetite so the plan of attack is to eat small amounts of food. Once again, avoid fatty foods and follow a similar eating plan to that for colds. Drink plenty of fluids, especially infusions with ginger.

Ginger & Honey Infusion

Serves 1

Nutrition	per serving
Calories (kcal)	37.1
Carbohydrate (g)	8.7
Protein (g)	0.5
Fat (g)	0.2
Fibre (g)	0.5

Ingredients
2cm fresh ginger, peeled and chopped
1 tsp lemon juice or cider vinegar
1 tsp honey
250ml hot water

Method
1. Place the ginger in a cup, along with lemon juice and honey.
2. Pour hot water into the cup and mix well.

Keeping PMS under control

If you or any men are sharing a house with a female, you will discover that PMS has very irrational tendencies. If you or anyone else you know has had the brunt of a PMS sufferer then help is at hand. Opposite is some advice to help the sufferer.

Stay away from sugary foods

A week before your period is due don't eat chocolate, biscuits or cakes and beware of hidden sugars in sauces, cereals, sweetened canned fruit and drinks. The craving for sweet foods is undoubtedly great but you must resist them because these foods will cause your sugar levels to drop and create mood swings.

Cut down on caffeine

Caffeine drinks including tea, coffee and fizzy drinks are known to cause headaches, breast tenderness and a feeling of nausea. These drinks only make your PMS worse, so limit them to one or two a day.

Eat regularly

By eating small meals every three to four hours you can alleviate the feelings of dizziness, sweating and mood swings, and can keep blood sugar levels constant.

Go high fibre

During menstruation a lot of oestrogen is produced, but by eating unprocessed carbohydrates (high in fibre) you can control the amount of oestrogen in your body. This means sugar levels are more constant so you won't feel as tired and out of energy as you usually do at this time. Eating two portions of vegetables and three portions of fruit each day also helps blood sugar and energy levels.

Up the minerals

The essential minerals for curbing the symptoms of PMS include zinc, iron (meat, eggs and nuts) and magnesium (wholemeal bread, wholegrain cereals, porridge, rice).

'A week before your period is due don't eat chocolate, biscuits or cakes and beware of hidden sugars in sauces, cereals, sweetened canned fruit and drinks.'

Eat more essential oils

Eating Omega 3 oils found in oily fish and Omega 6 found in pumpkin and sunflower seeds are known to stop breast tenderness.

PMS eating plan

Breakfast

- Fresh fruit salad with pumpkin and sunflower seeds.
- Porridge with dried apricots.
- Wholemeal toast with poached egg.

Lunch

- Sardines in tomato sauce with a wholemeal roll.
- Jacket potato and vegetable chilli.
- Couscous, pumpkin seed, pepper and broccoli salad.
- Avocado and egg salad.

Dinner

- Stir-fry pork strips with spinach and brown rice.
- Veggie burgers and brown rice.
- Chicken and cashew nut stir-fry.

Veggie Chilli

Serves 2

Nutrition	per serving
Calories (kcal)	257.9
Carbohydrate (g)	32.1
Protein (g)	10.9
Fat (g)	9.9
Fibre (g)	9.6

Great served with brown rice or as a topping for jacket potatoes

Ingredients
1 tbsp olive oil
1 medium onion, sliced thinly
1 garlic clove, peeled and sliced thinly
2 carrots, sliced into thin strips
½ pepper, seeded and diced
½ tsp chilli powder
½ tsp cumin powder
1 tbsp tomato purée
100g canned kidney beans, drained and washed
100g canned chickpeas, drained and washed
100g canned tomatoes
150ml vegetable stock

Method
1. Heat the oil in a large non-stick pan, add the onions and sauté for 5 minutes.
2. Add the garlic, carrot and pepper and cook for a further 3 - 4 minutes.
3. Add the spices and cook for 3 minutes to develop the flavour, followed by the tomato purée. Cook for another 2 minutes.
4. Add the kidney beans, chickpeas and tomatoes and mix well.
5. Pour in the vegetable stock and bring to the boil, then reduce the heat to simmer. Cook for 30 minutes and serve with brown rice.

Couscous & Pumpkin Seed Salad

Serves 4

Nutrition	per serving
Calories (kcal)	246.9
Carbohydrate (g)	24.4
Protein (g)	10.5
Fat (g)	12.3
Fibre (g)	3.0

Ingredients
1 tsp low fat margarine
1 x 110g packet couscous
200ml boiling hot water
75g pumpkin seeds
1 pepper, seeded and diced
125g broccoli, cut into small florets and steamed

Dressing
¼ tsp chilli powder
1 tbsp lemon juice
2 tsp olive oil
Salt and pepper (to taste)

Method
1. Melt the margarine in a saucepan.
2. Add the couscous and gently cook over a moderate heat for a minute.
3. Pour in boiling water and bring to the boil.
4. Remove from the heat, cover and stand for 5 minutes.
5. Return the pan to the heat for a minute, stirring with a fork to separate the grains.

6. Place the cooked couscous into a large bowl, add pumpkin seeds, pepper and steamed broccoli.
7. Mix together the dressing ingredients with a fork and pour over the couscous and vegetable mixture. Place in the fridge to chill.

Avocado & Egg Salad

Serves 2

Nutrition	per serving
Calories (kcal)	259.4
Carbohydrate (g)	5.6
Protein (g)	9.4
Fat (g)	22.4
Fibre (g)	4.0

Ingredients
2 handfuls of washed spinach leaves
½ red onion, sliced thinly
1 avocado, sliced with a sprinkle of lemon juice
2 hard boiled eggs, sliced
1 tsp olive oil
1 tsp vinegar
Salt and pepper (to season)

Method
1. Arrange the spinach leaves in a bowl, place sliced onion, avocado and eggs on top.
2. Put the olive oil, vinegar, salt and pepper into a clean jar with a lid and shake until well combined.
3. Pour the dressing over the salad.

Stir-Fry Pork Strips with Spinach

Serves 2

Nutrition	per serving
Calories (kcal)	452.3
Carbohydrate (g)	8.0
Protein (g)	45.1
Fat (g)	26.8
Fibre (g)	4.8

Ingredients

1 tbsp olive oil
200g pork fillet, cut into strips
1 garlic clove, peeled and sliced
2 spring onions, sliced
1 red chilli pepper, sliced thinly
5cm piece fresh ginger root, sliced
2 tbsp white sesame seeds
300g baby spinach leaves
2 tbsp light soy sauce
1 tbsp toasted sesame oil

Method

1. In a non-stick wok or large frying pan, heat the oil over a high heat and fry the pork strips.
2. Add the garlic, spring onions, chilli and ginger and continue to cook.
3. Stir in the sesame seeds and half of the spinach. Stir-fry for another minute and then add the soy sauce and sesame oil.
4. Turn the remaining uncooked spinach through the stir-fry and serve immediately with brown rice.

Veggie Burgers & Brown Rice

Serves 4

Nutrition	per serving
Calories (kcal)	369.4
Carbohydrate (g)	31.6
Protein (g)	10.4
Fat (g)	22.6
Fibre (g)	8.2

Ingredients
6 tbsp olive oil
1 onion, sliced thinly
1 celery stick, sliced thinly
1 garlic clove, peeled and crushed
1 leek, sliced thinly
1 x 400g can kidney beans, drained and washed
150g cooked brown rice
1 bunch flat-leaf parsley, chopped
Salt and pepper (to taste)

Method
1. Heat half the oil in a non-stick frying pan and add the onion, celery, garlic and leek. Fry gently until softened.
2. Add the kidney beans and rice and mash everything gently together.
3. Add the parsley and season with salt and pepper. Leave to cool before shaping into patties.
4. Heat the remaining olive oil in a frying pan and fry the patties for 2 - 3 minutes on each side until hot and golden.
5. Place patties in the centre of each plate and serve with a green salad.

Need2Know

Chicken & Cashew Nut Stir-Fry

Serves 2

Nutrition	per serving
Calories (kcal)	350.3
Carbohydrate (g)	15.9
Protein (g)	30.3
Fat (g)	18.4
Fibre (g)	2.3

Ingredients
2 tsp sunflower oil
200g skinless chicken breast, cut into small strips
1 onion, cut into wedges
1 clove garlic, peeled and crushed
¼ tsp chilli powder
50g cashew nuts

Sauce
2 tsp cornflour
125ml water
1 ½ tbsp soy sauce

Method
1. Mix together the cornflour with a small amount of water to form a paste. Then pour in the remaining water and soy sauce and mix together.
2. Using a non-stick wok or large frying pan heat up 1 teaspoon of oil, then add the chicken strips. Cook until the chicken is browned. Remove from the pan and place in a bowl.
3. Add the remaining teaspoon of oil to the pan/wok, heat up and add the onions. Sauté over a moderate heat for 5 minutes until the onions are softened.

4. Add the garlic and chilli powder and cook for a further minute.
5. Add the cashew nuts and stir through, cooking for 2 - 3 minutes.
6. Return the chicken strips to the pan and pour in soy sauce mixture. Boil until the sauce thickens. Serve with brown rice.

Summing Up

- Balance is the key word in maintaining good health.

- 'Superfoods' can have a positive impact on your health and should be eaten daily.

- For symptoms of stress eat more unrefined carbohydrates, do some exercise and also relax each day and take Arnica 6c.

- To deal with mood shifts eat more unrefined carbohydrates as well as protein foods high in tryptophan, vitamin B6 and C and minerals zinc and selenium.

- To sort out colds and coughs avoid eating carbohydrates and dairy foods, eat more foods rich in zinc and the vitamins B and C. Try and include lots of garlic and onions in your cooking and drink plenty of fluids.

- Deal positively with PMS by avoiding sugary foods and caffeine. Eat smaller meals based on more unrefined carbohydrates and up the minerals zinc and iron. For your essential oils, eat more Omega 3 and 6.

Chapter Five

The Big Breakfast

There's no doubt about it, breakfast by far is the most important meal of the day. A lot of people don't think it's that important and miss it altogether, yet by not eating it, you're not kick starting your metabolism.

After 10 to 12 hours of sleep the body needs energy. In other words, the body has no ready fuel (glucose) available, so movement and brain power are far slower than in regular breakfast eaters. In fact, you can lose 6% of your daily calorie allowance by missing breakfast because you haven't stoked up your metabolism. There is even research to show that you can lose weight by eating breakfast because you are less inclined to snack on fatty and sugary foods.

Getting into breakfasts

- Breakfast doesn't have to be cereal or toast; if you find it boring, think out of the box and have something savoury instead such as vegetable soup.

- Keep a good supply of fresh and dried fruit. A fruit bowl in your bedroom will encourage you to munch your breakfast while getting ready for lectures.

- If you prefer liquid breakfasts, you can squeeze your own fruit juices the night before and store them in the fridge so breakfast is ready for you.

- A warm breakfast doesn't require a lot of effort. While warming rolls in the oven, you can be getting washed and dressed.

'There's no doubt about it, breakfast by far is the most important meal of the day. A lot of people don't think it's that important and miss it altogether, yet by not eating it, you're not kick starting your metabolism.'

Some suggestions

Breakfasts on the go

- Fruity oaty yoghurt bars.
- Fruity raisin wheats with low fat yoghurt.
- Peanut butter/hummus on a bagel.
- Lush smoothie.

Hot and cold breakfasts

- Omelette with mushrooms and tomatoes.
- Low fat bacon buttie.
- Porridge with dried apricots.
- Mini pittas with lean ham and low fat soft cheese.
- Scrambled eggs on wholemeal toast.

Lazy weekend breakfasts

- Wholemeal soda bread, smoked salmon trimmings and poached egg.
- Low fat cooked breakfast with grilled bacon, sausage, tomato, poached egg and baked beans.
- Smoked haddock with spinach and poached egg.
- Wholewheat fruity piklets with fresh fruit and crème fraîche.

The morning after the night before

If you've ever had that fragile feeling after a night out on the tiles, the first thing your body craves is fatty and sugary foods, for example a fry up, a kebab or an iced donut. However, you actually need to eat the exact opposite to give your body a massive boost. Eating foods high in vitamin C, such as citrus fruits, berries and soft fruits like kiwis, will give your tired body an instant energy boost. Bananas are also great after a heavy night out because their natural sugar content helps to satisfy the need for sugary foods.

Recipes

Fruity Raisin Wheats with Low Fat Yoghurt

Serves 1

Nutrition	per serving
Calories (kcal)	285.5
Carbohydrate (g)	59.7
Protein (g)	8.8
Fat (g)	2.4
Fibre (g)	6.1

Ingredients
½ melon (galia or cantelope)
50g raisin wheats cereal
75g low fat yoghurt
50g strawberries, sliced

Method
1. Cut the melon in half and scoop out the seeds in the centre.
2. Fill with raisin wheats and top with yoghurt and sliced strawberries.

Need2Know

Lush Smoothie

Serves 1

Nutrition	per serving
Calories (kcal)	169.6
Carbohydrate (g)	35.3
Protein (g)	3.7
Fat (g)	1.0
Fibre (g)	6.8

Ingredients

1 banana, peeled and roughly chopped
½ can raspberries or a handful of fresh raspberries
2 tbsp low fat yoghurt
4 ice cubes

Method

1. Place all the ingredients in a blender or smoothie maker.
2. Blend together until smooth and pour into a glass.

Kiwi Shaker

Serves 1

Nutrition	per serving
Calories (kcal)	541.3
Carbohydrate (g)	127.7
Protein (g)	3.2
Fat (g)	0.8
Fibre (g)	11.7

If you're in a hurry or don't feel like eating breakfast, this smoothie is packed with vitamin C and minerals.

Ingredients
1 kiwi, peeled and roughly chopped
125g frozen summer mixed berries
1 banana, peeled and roughly chopped
125ml apple juice

Method
1. Place all the ingredients in a blender or smoothie maker.
2. Blend together until smooth and pour into a glass.

Mushroom & Tomato Omelette

Serves 1

Nutrition	per serving
Calories (kcal)	176.3
Carbohydrate (g)	4.9
Protein (g)	14.6
Fat (g)	11.0
Fibre (g)	1.9

Ingredients
Low fat spray
3 mushrooms, wiped and sliced thinly
2 eggs
1 tomato, sliced thinly
Salt and pepper (optional)

Method
1. Using a low fat spray, squirt 3 shots into a saucepan and heat up. Add the mushrooms and cook until soft. Keep to one side.
2. Whisk together the two eggs until frothy and season.
3. Preheat a non-stick frying pan with 3 sprays of low fat spray.
4. Pour in the eggs and cook until bubbles appear and the omelette sets. Tilt the pan away from you and loosen the sides.
5. Add the mushrooms and tomatoes on one half and then fold the other half over.

Low Fat Bacon Buttie

Serves 1

Nutrition	per serving
Calories (kcal)	237.6
Carbohydrate (g)	23.2
Protein (g)	15.0
Fat (g)	10.2
Fibre (g)	3.0

Ingredients
2 rashers lean back bacon
1 x wholemeal roll/bap
½ tsp low fat sunflower spread
Drizzle of tomato or brown sauce

Method
1. Place the bacon under an initially hot grill, then reduce the heat and grill for 5 - 8 minutes, turning the rashers over until crisp. You can also use a non-stick frying pan instead. Spray 2 - 3 shots of low fat spray into the pan and heat up.
2. Once the pan has reached the correct temperature (the spray becomes clear) place the bacon into the pan and fry for 5 - 8 minutes, turning each side over when cooked.
3. Cut a roll or bap in half and spread with low fat spread.
4. Remove any fat on the bacon and arrange in roll/bap. Add desired sauce.

Need2Know

Porridge

Serves 1

Nutrition	per serving
Calories (kcal)	192.0
Carbohydrate (g)	33.5
Protein (g)	8.4
Fat (g)	3.2
Fibre (g)	4.9

Ingredients
½ cup porridge oats (approx 50g)
1 ½ mugs water (Can do half milk, half water - optional)

Method
1. Add the oats and water to the pan, and cook over a moderate heat, stirring continuously. Bring to the boil for 1 minute, stirring.
2. Serve immediately with a topping of your choice, such as dried apricots.

Scrambled Eggs on Wholemeal Toast

Serves 1

Nutrition	per serving
Calories (kcal)	142.9
Carbohydrate (g)	12.1
Protein (g)	9.2
Fat (g)	6.8
Fibre (g)	1.8

Ingredients
1 egg
Salt and pepper (pinch)
1 tbsp milk
3 shots low fat spray
1 x slice wholemeal bread

Method
1. Whisk together the egg, salt, pepper and milk with a fork.
2. Using a low fat spray, squirt 3 shots into a saucepan and heat up.
3. Once the pan is hot, pour in the egg mixture.
4. Stir the egg mixture over a gentle heat until it forms soft curds. Spoon onto wholemeal toast.

Wholewheat Fruity Piklets with Crème fraîche

Makes 24

Nutrition	per piklet
Calories (kcal)	41.4
Carbohydrate (g)	6.8
Protein (g)	1.5
Fat (g)	0.9
Fibre (g)	0.9

You can make up the whole quantity and freeze into batches and use when required.

Ingredients
200g wholemeal self-raising flour
1 ½ tbsp honey
250ml semi-skimmed milk
1 egg, beaten
Low fat spray
50ml half-fat crème fraîche
50g raspberries or fruit of your choice.

Method
1. Sift the flour into a mixing bowl and form a well in the centre. Add the honey.
2. Pour in the milk and add egg to the well. Use a wooden spoon to gradually beat in the flour.
3. Once the mixture is well beaten, pour into a jug.
4. Spray 3 shots of low fat spray into a non-stick frying pan and heat until it becomes clear.

5. Put spoonfuls of the mixture on a hot pan. When bubbles appear on the surface of the piklets, turn over. Allow to brown on the other side and cook through.
6. Serve with crème fraîche and fresh soft fruit such as raspberries.

Poached Egg on Wholemeal Toast

Serves 1

Nutrition	per serving
Calories (kcal)	125.5
Carbohydrate (g)	10.8
Protein (g)	8.6
Fat (g)	5.6
Fibre (g)	1.5

Ingredients
6 drops vinegar
Salt (pinch)
1 egg
1 x slice wholemeal bread

Method
1. Boil 5cm of water in a saucepan. Add 6 drops of vinegar and a pinch of salt.
2. Break the egg into a cup and then gently slide into the saucepan.
3. Simmer on a low heat for 2 - 3 minutes, until the egg white sets.
4. Toast the bread and lay the poached egg on top.

Smoked Haddock, Spinach & Poached Egg

Serves 1

Nutrition	per serving
Calories (kcal)	155.7
Carbohydrate (g)	1.2
Protein (g)	22.7
Fat (g)	6.7
Fibre (g)	1.1

Ingredients
½ tsp low fat spread
50g spinach, washed in salt water with stalks removed
75g smoked haddock fillet
2 tbsp water
Lemon juice
1 egg
Salt and pepper (optional)

Method
1. Heat a non-stick frying pan and melt the margarine. Once the pan has reached temperature, add the spinach and sauté gently until cooked.
2. Meanwhile, wash the fish and arrange in a microwave dish. Add 2 tablespoons of water and a squeeze of lemon juice, cover with a lid or loose cling-film. Microwave on HIGH for 2 – 2 ½ minutes until cooked. Remove from the microwave and stand for 2 - 3 minutes.
3. Crack the egg into a lightly greased microwave dish. Prick the yolk and white, loosely cover the dish and microwave on HIGH for 40 – 50 seconds. Make sure the white around the yolk is cooked, if not then add extra cooking time. Remove from the microwave and stand.

4. Drain and place the haddock on a plate. Arrange the spinach on top followed by the poached egg and season with salt and pepper.

Oven-Baked Tomatoes

Serves 1

Nutrition	per serving
Calories (kcal)	154.6
Carbohydrate (g)	12.8
Protein (g)	3.6
Fat (g)	10.1
Fibre (g)	4.2

Ingredients

3 tomatoes, halved
½ tbsp olive oil
5g low fat margarine
½ clove garlic, peeled and chopped
1 tsp chopped parsley
1 tsp Worcestershire sauce
Salt (pinch)

Method

1. Preheat the oven to 190°C/375°F/Gas Mark 5
2. Put the tomatoes into an ovenproof dish with the cut sides facing upwards.
3. In a pan heat the oil and margarine. Add the garlic, parsley, Worcestershire sauce and salt.
4. Spoon over the tomatoes and bake for 15 minutes. Serve on wholemeal toast.

Homemade Muesli

Nutrition	per serving
Calories (kcal)	112.6
Carbohydrate (g)	21.3
Protein (g)	3.7
Fat (g)	1.9
Fibre (g)	2.6

Suggestion
- 75g chopped nuts or handful of seeds.

Ingredients
175g oatmeal
75g wheat germ
75g raisins
75g dried apple or dried fruit of your choice

Method
1. Combine all the ingredients and store in the fridge in an airtight container. Serve with milk or natural yoghurt.

Summing Up

- Breakfast is the most important meal of the day. If you miss it, you're not giving your metabolism that important kick start.

- Always keep a basket of fruit in your room - if you're in a rush, you can still munch while you get dressed.

- Be creative - breakfast does not need to be boring.

Chapter Six

Lunches

Eating lunch is necessary to sustain energy levels, especially to keep your concentration up during two hour lectures and in-depth tutorials. It is a good idea to not eat starchy cereals for lunch, such as pasta, as these can make you feel sleepy. You can, however, opt for other starches; wholemeal pitta bread, seeded bagels, breads and wraps are all good sources of carbohydrate energy and when combined with veggies and/or salad you're getting that extra boost you need. By planning and preparing foods in advance you can also save time and money.

■ You can prepare vegetables and fruit in advance by storing them in airtight containers. For example, you could mix together soft fruits, kiwis and some drained canned peaches. Once prepared, you can just grab and go with the fruit and vegetables you want. This is also useful for when you don't have time for lunch or time is limited.

■ Sandwiches, filled rolls and pitta bread can all be prepared in one go and kept in the fridge. Some can even be placed in the freezer, but you need to make sure the fillings can be frozen - lettuce and tomato based fillings are not suitable because their water content is too high.

■ Make protein, such as lean ham, chicken or turkey, the essential part of your lunch. If you're a veggie, hummus or guacamole with beans and vegetables are all good fillings. By including protein you send a feel good message to the brain.

■ If you're on the run in the morning get organised the night before and prepare your lunch in advance, so all you'll have to do is grab it and go!

■ In the summer get into freezing a few large bottles of sugar free squash diluted with water so you've always got plenty of cold liquid on hand. This will save on buying expensive drinks and will quench your thirst.

'It is a good idea to not eat starchy cereals for lunch, such as pasta, as these can make you feel sleepy.'

Lunch ideas

Tired and bored of the same sort of lunch fillings? Sandwiches, bread rolls, bagels, pitta/flat breads, whole wheat crisp breads, rice cakes and focaccia bread can be filled with the following combos to make them more interesting:

- Peanut butter with grated carrot.
- Low fat egg mayonnaise and watercress.
- Lean ham, low fat fromage frais and sliced tomato.
- Cottage or ricotta cheese with chopped dried fruit and a few chopped nuts.
- Hummus and cress.
- Low fat cheese and coleslaw.
- Grilled vegetables with mixed beans
- Tuna/salmon with salad and tomato.

You could also try:

- Toasties with baked beans, tuna and pesto.
- Split a muffin and bake with tomato purée topped with corn kernels, pineapple and a small sprinkling of cheese.

Other ideas

Homemade soup

Make up some fresh vegetable soup and store it in a small flask and serve with some wholemeal bread. If you make a larger quantity, it will do for lunch the next day.

Homemade pizza

Make up your own individual pizzas by making dough or using halved muffins. Prepare the pizzas in bulk and store them in the freezer and use them when required.

Salads

These needn't be boring. Try salads based on pasta, couscous or brown rice. Add veggie strips, lean meat pieces or sunflower and pumpkin seeds, along with low fat dressings. You can also try fruity salads with fresh berries, canned and drained fruits, seeds and a little low fat yoghurt.

Healthier lunch checklist

- Go easy on spreading margarine on bread or crisp breads.

- Add more salad to bulk up rolls, bagels and flat breads.

- Always use wholemeal bread and if you aren't into it, try having one slice white and the other wholemeal, then go all the way.

- Opt for reduced fat versions of mayonnaise and cheese.

- Choose low fat fillings such as lean ham, tuna, chicken or hummus.

- Add snacks such as plain popcorn (not sugared), dried fruit, bread sticks, rice cakes and fresh fruit.

Recipes

Homemade Pizza

Serves 4

Nutrition	per serving
Calories (kcal)	573.6
Carbohydrate (g)	69.6
Protein (g)	23.8
Fat (g)	22.4
Fibre (g)	6.0

Suggestion – any vegetables can be added as a topping.

Ingredients
Dough
7g dried yeast
1 tsp sugar
250ml hand-hot water
350g strong flour
1 tsp salt
1 tbsp olive oil

Topping
1 x 400g can chopped tomatoes
2 garlic cloves, peeled and crushed
1 tsp mixed herbs
1 tbsp olive oil
2 tbsp tomato purée
200g mushrooms, sliced thinly
1 red pepper, seeded and sliced into strips
2 tomatoes, sliced thinly

150g grated cheese
Salt and pepper (optional)

Method

1. Put the yeast and sugar into a jug and mix with 4 tablespoons of the water. Leave the yeast mixture in a warm place for 15 minutes or until frothy.
2. Mix the flour with the salt and make a well in the centre. Add the oil, the yeast mixture and the remaining water. Using a wooden spoon, mix to form a dough.
3. Knead the dough on a floured surface for 4 - 5 minutes.
4. Return the dough to the bowl, cover with a tea towel and leave until it has doubled in size.
5. Knead the dough for 2 minutes, stretching it with your hands, then roll out and place on an oiled baking tray. The dough should be reasonably thin (6mm approx) as it will rise during cooking.
6. Place the chopped tomatoes, garlic, herbs and olive oil in a large pan and simmer for 20 minutes. Stir in the tomato purée and leave to cool.
7. Spread the sauce over the pizza, top with mushrooms, pepper, tomatoes and cheese. Bake in a preheated oven set at 200°C/400°F/Gas Mark 6 for 25 minutes.

Prawn & Rocket Salad

Serves 2

Nutrition	per serving
Calories (kcal)	119.8
Carbohydrate (g)	8.4
Protein (g)	9.8
Fat (g)	5.6
Fibre (g)	2.1

Ingredients
1 tsp olive oil
75g cooked prawns
1 clove garlic, peeled and crushed
75g rocket leaves, washed
75g spinach, washed with stalks removed
½ red onion, sliced thinly

Dressing
1 tbsp sweet chilli sauce
2 tsp soy sauce
2 tsp lemon juice
1 tsp olive/sunflower oil

Method
1. Heat the oil in a non-stick frying pan over a medium heat. Add the prawns, followed by the garlic. Stir-fry for 2 minutes until just cooked.
2. Arrange the rocket, spinach and sliced onion slices on two plates.
3. Place prawns evenly on top of the salad.
4. Combine all the dressing ingredients together and drizzle over the salad.

Tomato & Basil Soup

Serves 4

Nutrition	per serving
Calories (kcal)	114.4
Carbohydrate (g)	15.9
Protein (g)	3.6
Fat (g)	4.3
Fibre (g)	2.9

Ingredients
1 tbsp olive oil
1 medium onion, sliced thinly
2 tbsp plain flour
5 medium sized tomatoes, peeled and chopped or 1 x 400g can chopped tomatoes
2 tbsp tomato purée
570ml vegetable stock
½ tsp sugar
¼ tsp salt
Bunch of fresh basil, chopped

Method
1. Heat the oil in a non-stick frying pan. Add the onions and fry until soft. Take off the heat and blend in the flour.
2. Return the pan to heat and cook for 2 minutes, stir in the tomatoes and tomato purée.
3. Add the stock, sugar, salt and basil.
4. Cover and simmer gently for 15 minutes.
5. Push the soup through a fine sieve with a spoon or use a blender or food processor.
6. Return the soup to the pan and heat up again for 2 - 3 minutes. Serve with a wholemeal crusty roll.

Leek & Potato Soup

Serves 4

Nutrition	per serving
Calories (kcal)	170.8
Carbohydrate (g)	20.8
Protein (g)	6.3
Fat (g)	7.1
Fibre (g)	4.3

Ingredients

1 tbsp olive oil
2 leeks, washed and sliced thinly
1 medium onion, sliced thinly
250g potatoes, peeled and diced
570ml water
300ml whole milk
Salt and pepper (to taste)

Method

1. Heat the oil in a large non-stick saucepan over a medium heat.
2. Add the leeks and onions and cook for 3 minutes, stirring frequently.
3. Add the potatoes and cook for a further minute before adding the water.
4. Place a lid on the pan and bring to the boil over a high heat. Turn down the heat and simmer for 20 minutes or until the potatoes are soft.
5. For a smoother soup put through a sieve, a blender or food processor.
6. Return to the pan and heat through, adding milk until desired consistency is reached.
7. Serve with a wholemeal crusty roll.

Need2Know

Lentil Soup

Serves 4

Nutrition	per serving
Calories (kcal)	159.7
Carbohydrate (g)	17.7
Protein (g)	6.6
Fat (g)	7.1
Fibre (g)	3.2

Ingredients
1 tbsp olive oil
1 medium onion, sliced thinly
15g butter
2 carrots, finely chopped
1.2 litres vegetable stock
75g split red lentils, rinsed
2 tbsp tomato purée
Salt and pepper (to taste)

Method
1. Heat the oil in a non-stick saucepan, add the onions and fry for 3 - 5 minutes, stirring until soft. Add the butter and carrots and fry for 5 more minutes, stirring all the time.
2. Add the stock, lentils and tomato purée. Bring to the boil, cover and simmer for 35 - 40 minutes until lentils are soft.
3. Serve with a wholemeal crusty roll.

Carrot & Coriander Soup

Serves 2

Nutrition	per serving
Calories (kcal)	336.5
Carbohydrate (g)	29.3
Protein (g)	5.9
Fat (g)	21.9
Fibre (g)	6.9

Ingredients
1 tbsp sunflower oil
1 small onion, sliced thinly
2 tsp ground coriander
500g carrots, thickly sliced
125ml vegetable stock
150ml half-fat crème fraîche
Salt and pepper (to taste)

Method
1. Heat the oil in a large non-stick saucepan and sauté the onions over a medium heat for 5 minutes or until soft.
2. Add the coriander and sauté for a further 2 minutes.
3. Add the carrots, mix and cook for 10 minutes.
4. Pour in the vegetable stock and bring to the boil. Cover and simmer for 30 - 40 minutes until the carrots are soft.
5. Purée the soup using a blender, food processor or push through a sieve until smooth. Return to the pan.
6. Stir in the crème fraîche and gently reheat the soup.
7. Serve with a wholemeal crusty roll.

Tuna & Chickpea Salad

Serves 4

Nutrition	per serving
Calories (kcal)	336.7
Carbohydrate (g)	22.8
Protein (g)	21.5
Fat (g)	17.2
Fibre (g)	7.4

Ingredients
1 x 400g can of chickpeas, drained
1 medium onion, sliced thinly
1 celery stick, sliced thinly
1 clove garlic, peeled and finely chopped
2 tbsp finely chopped parsley
1 ½ tbsp red wine vinegar
4 tbsp olive/vegetable oil
Salt and pepper (pinch)
1 x 185g can tuna, drained
2 medium tomatoes, sliced thinly
Lettuce leaves to garnish

Method
1. In a large bowl, mix together the chickpeas, onion, celery, garlic and parsley. Add the vinegar, oil, salt and pepper and mix well.
2. Break the tuna into chunks and add to the salad. Add the tomatoes. Serve on the lettuce leaves.

Hummus

Serves 4

Nutrition	per serving
Calories (kcal)	253.0
Carbohydrate (g)	10.8
Protein (g)	7.7
Fat (g)	19.9
Fibre (g)	3.6

If you make more than you need, store in the fridge for lunch the next day!

Ingredients
1 x 410g can chickpeas, rinsed and drained
4 tbsp water or vegetable stock
2 large cloves garlic
3 tbsp tahini
3 tbsp lemon juice
Salt (to taste)
1 tbsp olive oil

Garnish
Chopped fresh parsley
Olive oil
Pine nuts, fried
Paprika

Method
1. Heat the chickpeas and the water or stock in a saucepan.
2. When warmed through, place the chickpeas and half the stock or water in a food processor. Blend until roughly combined. Add the garlic, tahini and lemon juice and a couple of pinches of salt and blend again.
3. Add the olive oil and blend again until hummus is the desired texture.
4. Serve on wholemeal bread topped with a drizzle of olive oil, parsley, fried pine nuts and a sprinkling of paprika.

Bacon & Pasta Bake

Serves 2

Nutrition	per serving
Calories (kcal)	784.8
Carbohydrate (g)	111.9
Protein (g)	35.3
Fat (g)	22.0
Fibre (g)	14.9

Ingredients
2 rashers lean back bacon
250g whole wheat pasta (approx)
1 x 295g can condensed chicken soup
Whole milk
1 x 215g can sweetcorn
50g grated cheese

Method
1. Preheat the oven to 190°C/375°C/Gas Mark 5
2. Cook the bacon (see methods on page 136).
3. Cook the pasta (see methods on page 35).
4. Drain the pasta and return to the saucepan. Add the soup and using the empty can, fill with milk and add.
5. Add the sweetcorn and mix.
6. Chop the bacon into small strips and add.
7. Put the ingredients into a casserole dish and sprinkle the cheese on top.
8. Cook for 20 minutes until cheese is golden. Serve with salad.

Spanish Tortilla

Serves 4

Nutrition	per serving
Calories (kcal)	519.2
Carbohydrate (g)	48.3
Protein (g)	20.1
Fat (g)	27.5
Fibre (g)	5.1

Adapt this and use any vegetables or cheese that needs using up!

Ingredients
1kg potatoes, sliced thinly
4 tbsp vegetable oil
1 medium onion, sliced thinly
2 garlic cloves, peeled and crushed
1 green pepper, seeded and sliced
2 tomatoes, chopped
6 eggs, beaten
2 tbsp mixed herbs
Salt and pepper (optional)
50g grated cheese

Method
1. Parboil the potatoes in a saucepan of lighted salted boiling water. Drain well and leave to one side.
2. Heat the oil in a large non-stick frying pan and add the potato and onions. Sauté over a low heat, stirring constantly for 5 minutes until the potatoes have browned.
3. Add the garlic, pepper and tomatoes. Mix well.
4. Pour in the eggs, herbs and season to taste. Cook for 12 – 13 minutes, until the underside is cooked through.

5. Remove the frying pan from the heat, add the cheese and finish cooking under a medium grill for 5 - 7 minutes or until the mixture is set and looks golden brown.
6. Cut the tortilla into wedges and serve with salad.

Roasted Vegetables & Couscous

Serves 4

Nutrition	per serving
Calories (kcal)	390.0
Carbohydrate (g)	63.2
Protein (g)	13.7
Fat (g)	9.6
Fibre (g)	6.6

Ingredients
2 tbsp vegetable oil
1 large onion, chopped into wedges
1 carrot chopped into chunks
1 parsnip chopped into chunks
2 tomatoes, peeled and chopped into wedges
2 courgettes, chopped in half
1 red pepper, seeded and chopped
275g couscous
500ml vegetable stock
Salt and pepper (optional)

Method

1. Preheat the oven to 240°C/475°F/Gas Mark 9.
2. Put the vegetables in a roasting tin and coat with the oil. Roast in the oven for approximately 30 minutes or until the vegetables are cooked.
3. While the vegetables are cooking, prepare the couscous. Pour into a mixing bowl, add the stock, fork through, cover and leave for 5 minutes until the water has been absorbed.
4. Place the roasted vegetables on a layer of couscous and serve.

Baked Stuffed Tomatoes

Serves 2

Nutrition	per serving
Calories (kcal)	184.8
Carbohydrate (g)	14.7
Protein (g)	5.7
Fat (g)	11.8
Fibre (g)	2.4

Ingredients
2 large firm tomatoes
1 clove garlic, peeled and crushed
¼ tsp dried basil
1 ½ tbsp fine dry breadcrumbs
1 ½ tbsp finely chopped parsley
1 tbsp olive/vegetable oil
1 ½ tbsp grated cheese
Salt and pepper (optional)

Method
1. Preheat the oven to 200°C/400°F/Gas Mark 6.
2. Cut the tomatoes in half crosswise and remove seeds with a teaspoon.
3. In a small bowl, combine the garlic, basil, breadcrumbs, parsley, oil, cheese, salt and pepper. Spoon the mixture into the tomato halves.
4. Place the tomatoes in a greased shallow casserole dish and bake for 10 - 12 minutes. The tomatoes should be tender but hold their shape.

Summing Up

- Eating lunch is necessary to sustain energy levels.
- Lunch doesn't have to be boring – remember to be creative!
- By planning meals in advance you can save time and money.
- Follow the healthier lunch checklist.

Chapter Seven

Cooking Tea the Low Fat Way

The secret to getting to grips with low fat cooking is very simple; firstly choose a healthy recipe with the ingredients that are available to you, collect the equipment and ingredients that you need, weigh and measure them, prepare the food and then just cook it.

There's no need to get into a stress if mistakes are made because, more often than not, it can be put right. If you've cooked meals before, you can be more ambitious, but if you're a beginner don't choose recipes that are too complicated. Once you've mastered a couple of recipes you'll have the confidence to prepare more complicated dishes. The trick is to take things one step at a time.

'There's no need to get into a stress if mistakes are made because, more often than not, it can be put right.'

Cooking bacon and sausages

Bacon and sausages both contain saturated fat so they don't require any more fat added to them. The low fat cooking approach is to grill or pan-fry (non-stick pan) them using olive or sunflower oil spray or using just a tiny amount of fat heated up to moisten the meat. Not only does this control the amount of added fat but it doesn't compromise on flavour. It is advisable to cut off any visible fat that may be around bacon with either a knife or scissors. Never be tempted to cook sausages or bacon at high temperatures as the outside is browned too quickly and the inside isn't cooked and often can be raw. This can result in serious food poisoning.

Cooking sausages the low fat way

Cooked on the hob
2 sausages
3 sprays low fat spray

1. Squirt the spray oil onto a non-stick frying pan and heat until the fat is slightly bubbling. Place the sausages in the frying pan and cook for about 5 minutes, turning them so that each side gets browned evenly.
2. Reduce the heat and cook for a further 12 - 15 minutes until the sausages are cooked through.

Cooked under the grill
1. Line the grill tray with aluminium foil (shiny side up) and place sausages (no need to prick them) on the rack. Place on a medium heat on the lowest level of the grill.
2. Grill for 10 - 15 minutes, turning alternately until browned and cooked through.

Cooking bacon the low fat way

Cooked on the hob
2 rashers back bacon, fat trimmed off
3 sprays low fat spray

1. Preheat a non-stick frying pan with a little oil and wait until it bubbles.
2. Place the bacon rashers into the frying pan and cook for about 7 minutes, turning each rasher over. Once one side is brown, turn it over to the other side and do the same.

Cooked under the grill

1. Line the grill rack with aluminium foil (shiny side up) and place the bacon on it. Place on a medium heat on the lowest level of the grill.
2. Grill for 5 - 7 minutes (depending on how crispy you want it), turning each rasher over. Once one side is brown and crispy turn it over to the other side and do the same.

Roasting chicken

Roasting a whole chicken isn't as daunting as it might initially appear. Chicken is considered to be a high risk food, so you need to take care as to how it is defrosted (if frozen), stored in the fridge and the length of cooking time required. The majority of chickens don't contain salmonella, but care still needs to be taken in these areas.

Easy steps to roasting chicken

▪ If you are cooking a whole chicken from frozen make sure it's thoroughly defrosted and take out the giblets in the plastic bag found inside the cavity. If you buy an oven-ready chicken you won't have to do this.

▪ Always check the weight of the chicken you're cooking. This can be found on the packaging. As a rule, for every 450g/1lb allow 20 minutes and 20 minutes extra cooking time (see page 23). For example, a 1.35kg/3lb chicken will require 1 hour and 20 minutes cooking time in total. To test whether it's cooked properly the juices need to run clear from the meat and there shouldn't be any pinkish bit near the meat and bone.

▪ There are several ways to roast chicken using low fat cooking techniques. The best low fat method is to use a roasting tin with a lid or a roasting bag which keeps all the juices in, making the chicken very tender. Another method is to use a roasting pan lined with baking paper and then covered with aluminium foil.

▪ Chicken can be seasoned any number of ways but the simplest method is to season it with salt and pepper, or you can add other herbs and seasonings such as mixed herbs or chicken seasoning. Even a whole lemon can be stuffed into the chicken's cavity which creates a delicious and tender tasting roast chicken.

■ Chicken pieces require a shorter cooking time and are more convenient to prepare when time is short. Chicken drumsticks, thighs and quarters are just as delicious to eat when seasoned well.

Roasted chicken in the oven

1. Wash the chicken, remove the giblets and pat dry with paper kitchen towel.
2. Calculate the weight of the chicken and preheat the oven to 180°C/350°F/ Gas Mark 4.
3. Season the chicken with salt, pepper and other herbs and spices.
4. Place the seasoned chicken on a lined (baking paper) roasting pan and cover loosely with aluminium foil (shiny side inside). Make sure that the foil is tight around the pan edges.
5. Roast for the required time and baste (using a dessert spoon or pastry brush) the chicken occasionally to keep the chicken moist. Remove the foil half an hour before the end of the cooking time.
6. Once the chicken is cooked you can test it by seeing if the juices run clear and checking the flesh isn't pinkish near the bone. Take the chicken out of the oven and cover with foil and allow to stand for 10 minutes (this makes it easier to carve).

Roasted chicken pieces in the oven

1. Preheat the oven to 180°C/350°F/Gas Mark 4.
2. Wash and trim the excess fat from the chicken pieces. Pat them dry with paper kitchen towel.
3. In a bowl or freezer bag, add the chicken pieces, the oil and seasonings (e.g. salt, pepper, chilli powder, garlic or herbs) and mix/shake well so that each chicken piece is fully coated.
4. Place the chicken pieces onto a roasting pan lined with baking paper.
5. Roast in the oven for 30 – 35 minutes.

Old favourites with a low fat twist

Low Fat Spag Bol

Serves 4

Nutrition	per serving
Calories (kcal)	337.7
Carbohydrate (g)	37.0
Protein (g)	22.0
Fat (g)	11.4
Fibre (g)	5.6

Ingredients
1 tbsp sunflower/olive oil
1 medium onion, chopped finely
1 clove garlic, peeled and crushed
½ tsp thyme and ½ tsp basil or 1 tsp mixed herbs
¼ tsp chilli powder (optional)
250g lean minced beef
1 tbsp tomato purée
2 tomatoes, chopped or ½ can tomatoes, chopped
125ml water
1 tsp salt
200g whole wheat spaghetti

Method
1. Heat the oil in non-stick pan and add the onions. Sauté for 5 - 8 minutes on a medium heat until soft.
2. Add the garlic and sauté for a minute, add the herbs and chilli. Cook for 1 minute.
3. Add the beef and cook for 10 minutes.

4. Add the tomato purée, mix in well and cook for 2 minutes.
5. Add the tomatoes, salt and water. Bring up to temperature then reduce to a simmer and cook for 30 minutes.
6. Cook the spaghetti in boiling salted water for 15 - 20 minutes or until tender. Drain and keep warm.
7. Pour the sauce over the spaghetti and serve immediately.

Low Fat Cottage Pie

Serves 4

Nutrition	per serving
Calories (kcal)	311.1
Carbohydrate (g)	34.7
Protein (g)	19.2
Fat (g)	11.3
Fibre (g)	3.4

Ingredients
1 tbsp sunflower oil
1 medium onion, chopped finely
250g lean minced beef
1 tbsp flour
2 tomatoes, chopped
1 tbsp tomato sauce
1 tbsp Worcestershire sauce
1 tsp mixed herbs
½ tsp salt
3 shakes pepper
125ml beef or chicken stock

Mashed potato
4 medium potatoes, peeled and cut into pieces
3 tbsp semi-skimmed milk, warmed in the microwave
1 tbsp half-fat crème fraîche
Salt and pepper (optional)

Method

1. Preheat the oven to 180°F/350°F/Gas Mark 4.
2. Place the prepared potatoes into a saucepan and cover with water. Bring to the boil and reduce the heat to a simmer with the lid on. Cook for 15 - 20 minutes until soft.
3. When the potatoes are soft (test with a fork), remove from the heat and drain. Mash the potatoes and add crème fraîche, salt and pepper (to taste) and warmed milk. Mix together until light and fluffy and put to one side.
4. Heat the oil in a large non-stick pan and add the onions. Sauté for 5 - 8 minutes on a medium heat until soft.
5. Add the meat and cook until browned.
6. Stir in the flour and mix for 1 - 2 minutes until lightly browned.
7. Add the tomatoes, tomato sauce, Worcestershire sauce, herbs, salt, pepper and stock. Cook for 10 minutes, then reduce the heat and simmer for 20 minutes.
8. Once cooked, place into an ovenproof dish and arrange the mashed potatoes on top.
9. Place in the oven for 25 - 30 minutes until brown.

Need2Know

Low Fat Bangers & Mash

Serves 2

Nutrition	per serving
Calories (kcal)	663.1
Carbohydrate (g)	71.1
Protein (g)	21.2
Fat (g)	33.0
Fibre (g)	5.7

Ingredients
1 tsp sunflower oil
4 sausages
1 medium onion, cut into rings
2 tbsp instant gravy mix
280ml boiling water

Mashed potato
4 medium potatoes, peeled and cut into pieces
1 tbsp half-fat crème fraîche
Salt and pepper (optional)
3 tbsp semi-skimmed milk, warmed in the microwave

Method
1. Place the oil in a non-stick frying pan and heat up. Place the sausages in the pan and cook for 10 minutes. Turn regularly to make sure all sides are browned.
2. While waiting for the sausages, place the prepared potatoes into a saucepan and cover with water. Bring to the boil and reduce the heat to a simmer with the lid on. Cook for 15 – 20 minutes until soft.
3. When the potatoes are soft (test with a fork), remove from the heat and drain.
4. Mash the potatoes and add crème fraîche, salt, pepper (to taste) and warmed milk. Mix together until light and fluffy.

5. Add the onions to the sausages and sauté over a medium heat. Do this for 10 minutes, until soft. Once cooked through, remove from the heat and keep warm.
6. Blend together the instant gravy mix with boiling water and whisk until smooth. Pour the gravy mixture onto the sausages, add the onions and cook through. Remove from the heat and keep warm.
7. Serve the mash potatoes with warmed bangers and gravy.

Something different for tea

Chicken & Sweet Chilli Stir-Fry

Serves 2

Nutrition	per serving
Calories (kcal)	199.5
Carbohydrate (g)	12.6
Protein (g)	22.8
Fat (g)	6.6
Fibre (g)	3.7

Ingredients

150g chicken, cut into strips
2 tsp soy sauce
2 tsp sunflower oil
1 small onion, cut into wedges
1 clove garlic, peeled and crushed
1 carrot, cut into small strips
150g broccoli florets
50ml cold water
2 tsp sweet chilli sauce
1 tsp cornflour and extra water to form a paste

Method

1. Combine the chicken strips with the soy sauce. Allow to stand for 15 minutes while preparing other ingredients.
2. Heat 1 teaspoon of oil in a large non-stick frying pan. Add the chicken and brown for 8 - 10 minutes. Remove from the pan and place in a dish and set aside.

3. Add the second teaspoon of oil to the pan, heat and add the onions, garlic and carrots and stir-fry for 2 minutes.
4. Add the broccoli and water. Cover the pan and cook until the vegetables are tender but not soft.
5. Add the sweet chilli sauce, followed by the dissolved cornflour and water paste and mix well.
6. Return the cooked chicken to the pan and heat up until the sauce boils and thickens. Serve with rice.

Chickpea & Spinach Curry

Serves 1

Nutrition	per serving
Calories (kcal)	393.2
Carbohydrate (g)	50.5
Protein (g)	21.3
Fat (g)	12.4
Fibre (g)	13.6

Ingredients
1 tsp sunflower oil
1 small onion, sliced thinly
Salt (pinch)
1 tsp curry powder
1 x 215g can chickpeas, drained
50g spinach (fresh or frozen), chopped
200g tomatoes, chopped
1 tbsp low fat natural yoghurt

Method
1. Heat the oil in a non-stick saucepan or wok and sauté the onions until soft for 5 - 8 minutes. Add a tiny amount of salt to the onions to draw out some of the juices.
2. Add the curry powder and cook for another minute.
3. Add the chickpeas and spinach and cook for 3 - 4 minutes. Next add the tomatoes and cook for 5 minutes.
4. Stir in the low fat natural yoghurt, gently warm and serve.

Chicken Wraps

Serves 2

Nutrition	per serving
Calories (kcal)	577.2
Carbohydrate (g)	73.3
Protein (g)	44.2
Fat (g)	11.9
Fibre (g)	6.9

Ingredients
2 skinless chicken breasts, cut into strips
1 tsp chicken seasoning
1 tsp olive oil
1 small onion, chopped finely
50g mushrooms, sliced
1 pepper, seeded and cut into strips
4 wraps
2 tbsp tomato salsa
2 tbsp low fat natural yoghurt

Method
1. Cut the chicken into bite size pieces or strips and sprinkle with chicken seasoning in a small bowl.
2. Heat the olive oil in a large non-stick frying pan and sauté the onions for 5 minutes.
3. Add the seasoned chicken and cook for 5 minutes.
4. Add the mushrooms and peppers and cook for a further 5 minutes. Make sure the chicken is thoroughly cooked.
5. Warm the wraps in the microwave on HIGH for 50 seconds.
6. To assemble: open out the wrap, fill with the cooked chicken and vegetable mixture, spread ½ tablespoon of tomato salsa and finish off with ½ tablespoon of low fat natural yoghurt and roll up.

Vegetable Toad-in-the-Hole

Serves 4

Nutrition	per serving
Calories (kcal)	316.4
Carbohydrate (g)	33.6
Protein (g)	10.4
Fat (g)	15.8
Fibre (g)	3.2

Ingredients
Batter

100g plain flour
Salt (pinch)
2 eggs, beaten
200ml whole milk
2 tbsp mustard
2 tbsp vegetable/olive oil

Vegetable filling

25g low fat sunflower spread
2 garlic cloves, peeled and crushed
1 medium onion, cut into chunks
75g carrots, sliced thinly
50g green beans
50g canned sweetcorn, drained
2 tomatoes, seeded and chunked
1 tsp mustard
1 tbsp mixed herbs
Salt and pepper (to season)

Method

1. Preheat the oven to 200°C/400°F/Gas Mark 6.
2. Sift the flour and a pinch of salt into a bowl. Beat in the eggs and milk to make a batter. Stir in the mustard and leave to stand.
3. Pour the oil into a shallow ovenproof dish and heat in the oven for 10 minutes.
4. To make the filling, melt the margarine in a non-stick frying pan and sauté the garlic and onions, stirring constantly for 2 minutes. Cook the carrots and beans in a saucepan of boiling water until tender. Drain well.
5. Add the sweetcorn and tomatoes to the frying pan, followed by the mustard and herbs. Season well and add the carrots and beans.
6. Remove the dish from the oven and pour in the batter. Spoon the vegetables into the centre, return to the oven and cook for 30 - 35 minutes. Serve immediately.

Takeaways

The low down on takeaways and eating out

As much as you try to live the budget conscious student lifestyle, there will be odd times when you'll eat out or have a takeaway. Eating out and having that occasional takeaway is great fun because you can enjoy getting together with your friends, but you need to bear in mind that some options are higher in fat than others. Here's a guide to steer you down the healthy eating route so you don't over do it.

Chinese

Chinese food can potentially be healthy if you make the right choices.

Good Chinese food choices

- Boiled rice or noodles are healthier low fat choices because they're full of fibre and carbohydrates. Chow mein is a good choice because it's largely based on noodles.

- Many dishes are based on chicken, tofu, fish or seafood, all of which are low in saturated fat. Healthy options include chicken with pineapple, prawn chop suey and sweet and sour bean curd.

- Stir fried vegetables are the best choice because very little oil is used in the stir-frying process without compromising any flavour.

Chinese food to go easy on

- Avoid deep fries, battered side dishes such as dim sims, wontons, crispy duck and deep fried seaweed. Even spring rolls and prawn crackers are full of fat.

- Unless you are vegetarian, try and avoid eating cashews and peanuts in dishes.

- Keep away from coconut rice or anything with coconut milk.

- Don't order dishes that have sauces such as black bean, yellow bean, sweet and sour, hoisin and plum sauce.

Indian

There's no getting away from it - Indian dishes are generally high in fat. However, there are a few dishes that you can eat without worrying too much.

Good Indian food choices

- Tikka and tandoori dishes are the best choices mainly because of how they are cooked. Tikka meat is dry roasted with very little, if any, fat. Tandoori dishes are marinated in yoghurt and spices and then baked in a clay oven.

- Vegetable dishes and lentil or bean based curries (dahl) are low fat and are a healthy option that is both tasty and filling.

- Basmati rice has a delicious and pleasant flavour. It is also a very good low fat option and is the perfect partner to a low fat Indian meal. Pilau rice is fried in oil and should be avoided.

Indian foods to go easy on

- Keep away from korma and biryani dishes because they're loaded with cream and oil.

'Many Chinese dishes are based on chicken, tofu, fish or seafood, all of which are low in saturated fat.'

- Nan bread and chappatis are always a huge temptation and you can easily get carried away tucking into a pile of them.

- Like Chinese food, Indian dishes such as samosas and bhajas are deep fried and loaded with fat.

- Don't forget that dips such as riata and mango chutney are also high in calories.

Pizzerias

Pizzas are deceptively high in fat even though they don't taste or look particularly fatty.

Good pizza choices

- Small and thin crusted pizzas are the way to go. They contain far less fat than the larger stuffed crusted pizzas.

- In most pizzerias you can create your own pizza. By choosing a small, thin crusted pizza with simple toppings such as tomatoes, mushrooms, onions, peppers, sweetcorn and a little lean chicken, you can greatly cut down on the fat.

- Share a pizza with a friend and bulk up the rest of the meal with a salad on the side. This is possibly the healthiest option, but be careful not to go crazy with the salad dressings.

Pizzas to go easy on

- Keep away from starters in pizzerias. Garlic bread, deep fried, crumbed mushrooms and chicken wings are all loaded with fat.

- Avoid toppings such as salami and pepperoni and opt for tuna, sweetcorn and olives instead.

- Inevitably cheese is part of the pizza deal. Avoid pizzas such as quatro formaggio (pizza with four cheeses). If you love the cheesy pizza experience you can get the same flavour sensation by sprinkling a teaspoon of parmesan cheese on top of your pizza. Parmesan cheese is very high in calcium compared to cheddar and mozzarella cheese.

The chippie

A great part of British culture but it's quite limited in healthy choices.

Good chippie choices

- Fish coated in batter is very high in fat so you should choose a smaller piece rather than a larger one. You can also remove the cooked batter and just eat the fish. Grilled fish cakes are also a good healthy option.

- Choose thicker cut chips as these absorb less fat or go for a smaller portion of chips.

- Mushy peas, a slice of bread (no butter) and a small piece of battered fish is a more nutritious alternative than fish and chips. Another option is to choose a sausage or chicken (without the skin).

Chippie foods to go easy on

- Eating meat pies, sausage rolls and pasties are not good choices. A steak and kidney pie is a fatty blow out when combined with chips.

- Curry sauce and gravy are not good options. If you're a chip 'dipper' go for tomato ketchup instead.

- Bits of batter on the bottom of the chip bag. These are absolutely lethal and full of saturated fat. Always take your chips out of the bag, put them on a plate and get rid of the bag straightaway so you don't get tempted!

'Bits of batter on the bottom of the chip bag. These are absolutely lethal and full of saturated fat.'

Burger joints

McDonalds, Burger King and KFC are takeaway favourites, and many of these establishments have made an effort to offer healthier food alternatives.

Good choices

- Go for plain burgers instead of double burgers. These are a big no, no as they're loaded with saturated fat.

- Check out how the burgers are cooked. Most burgers are cooked in loads of fat, but there are some that are flame-grilled or barbecued and have slightly less fat.

- Choose fruit juices instead of milkshakes loaded with sugar. Avoid diet soft drinks as these are full of sugar and drinking too many will effect calcium absorption.

Go easy on

- Mayonnaise is piled onto burgers, so you can ask them to leave it off or replace it with more lettuce, fresh tomato or gerkins.

- Chips from burger joints tend not to offer very much nutritionally because they soak up lots of fat – so either don't have them or order only a very small portion. Some places offer good alternatives such as corn on the cob or baked beans.

- Stay well clear of burger joint desserts - they are lethal. Try some of the fresh fruit options instead.

Pub food

This option provides a wider selection of healthier options.

Good pub food choices

- You can never go wrong with a jacket potato, provided it's not got butter or margarine on it. Be careful with the amount of cheese though, as this can be very fatty. It's much better to stick with baked beans or tuna and salad.

- Stick to salad platters that are piled high with salad and choose tuna, lean ham, chicken, turkey or egg salad. Avoid Ploughman's lunches with cheese as the amount of fat featured on the plate is usually enough for the week's allowance.

- When it comes to ordering sandwiches you need to control the fillings you have. Make sure you have your sandwich filled with plenty of salad and avoid ready made fillings that are mixed with mayonnaise or grated cheese.

- Make sensible meat choices and don't over do it. When choosing steak, a 5 - 6oz is more than enough for anyone. Be sure also to trim off any fat around the edges. This is saturated fat and an artery killer!

- Low fat meats such as chargrill tuna steak, gammon steak, marinated chicken and salmon are available in many pubs and are healthy options.

Pub foods to go easy on

- Scotch eggs, pork pies and quiche are fatty foods. If you like the traditional pub fare, try meat dishes topped with potato, such as shepherd's pie or cottage pie.

- Steer clear of oil and mayonnaise based dressings. If you simply cannot do without a little dressing then take only one sachet and remain in control - if you don't, you'll be on the slippery slope.

- Keep away from anything on the pub menu that says 'creamy' or 'rich' - this simply equals fatty. Choose horseradish, tartare sauce or tomato ketcup instead.

- Chips are featured regularly as an accompaniment to most pub meals, so wherever possible go for jacket or boiled new potatoes without butter.

Italian food

This possibly has the widest selection of healthy options because most of the dishes are based on tomatoes, olive oil, herbs and pasta.

Good Italian food choices

- Stick to dishes such as arrabiata, marinara, napoletana and puttanesca. These Italian dishes are either based on tomatoes, vegetables or seafood, so they are less fatty.

- Risotto is a rice based dish and is a great alternative to pasta. It fills you up because it usually contains veggies.

Italian foods to go easy on

- Creamy sauces such as carbonara should be avoided because they contain butter and cream. Also try and avoid lasagne, cannelloni or any dish that is 'al forno' as these dishes are layered with cheese sauces.

- Bruschetta, breadsticks and focaccia breads. These are served with oil, so it's best to avoid them and opt for a side salad instead.

- Starters such as garlic mushrooms and antipasto dishes are very high in fat. If you are hungry and desperately want to eat a starter, opt for minestrone soup or parma ham and melon.

French food

French food is very restrictive in terms of healthier options as most dishes are based on creamy sauces and contain butter.

Good French food choices

- Go for grilled sole, a bowl of vichysoisse (potato and leek) or consommé soup (clear and tasty) as these contain the least amount of fat.

- Order crudités (chopped raw vegetable slices) without rich dips and rich sauces. These will fill you up between courses. Also choose extra vegetables (without butter or other dressings) as a side dish with your main course.

French foods to go easy on

- Stay well clear of the super rich puddings such as crème brulee, crème caramel and chocolate mousse and go for sorbets, fresh fruit salad or a scoop of ice cream instead.

- French bread is lethal. You can have a couple of small pieces but resist the temptation of having the whole bread stick!

'Stay well clear of the super rich puddings such as crème brulee, crème caramel and chocolate mousse and go for sorbets, fresh fruit salad or a scoop of ice cream instead.'

156

Greek food

Greek food has many healthy, savoury dishes to choose from.

Good Greek food choices

- Many of the fish dishes are grilled or baked. Dishes such as plaki are tomato based with onion and garlic, and grilled sardines are also good because they provide you with the essential Omega 3 fatty oils.

- Meze is a popular starter where you have a choice of different small starter dishes. Keep to tsatziki, hummus, a couple of olives and pitta bread.

- All kinds of kebabs. These are very good choices as they are grilled and usually contain several skewered veggies along with the meat.

Greek foods to go easy on

- Greek salad as it contains feta cheese and has oil drizzled on top.

- Dolmades (stuffed vine leaves) which are saturated in oil. Be careful also of moussaka, a Greek favourite but full of fat because it contains cream and cheese.

Mexican

Mexican food does have a selection of healthy options to choose from.

Good Mexican food choices

- Dishes such as ceviche (seafood salad with lime), gazpacho (chilled tomato and cucumber soup), pico de gallo (tomatoes with onions and hot peppers) and tomato salsa (chopped tomatoes with onion and chilli) are all low fat dishes to choose.

- Many of the dishes are based around beans and pulses which are high in fibre. Some good choices include black bean soup and refried beans.

- Go for the soft (not fried) tortilla stuffed with chicken or beans. These contain less fat than the usual tortillas.

Mexican foods to go easy on

- Fajitas, enchiladas and chimichangas should be avoided as they are full of fat. The tortillas are fried in oil and covered either in a sauce or cheese or both!

- Nachos, tacos and tortillas are usually smothered in sour cream and guacamole. You can control the amount you have by asking for the dips to be halved and placed into separate small dishes or share them with a friend.

Summing Up

- Cooking healthy meals is simple.

- If you've cooked meals before, you can be more ambitious, but if you're a beginner don't choose recipes that are too complicated.

- Eating out and having that occasional takeaway is great fun because you can enjoy getting together with your friends, but you need to bear in mind that some options are higher in fat than others.

Chapter Eight

Puddings

There's no escaping the fact that almost everyone loves a pudding. No meal seems complete without one and it finishes off the whole eating experience. The obvious healthy pudding that springs to mind is a fresh fruit salad. It would seem the most nutritious way to end a meal, but sometimes you do like something that is more indulgent. Indulgence doesn't have to equal unhealthy.

The basis of a good, tasty, healthy pudding is to avoid fat laden pastries or cream. These are loaded with saturated fat (not so good). Good substitutes instead are fatless sponges, meringues, low fat fromage frais and yoghurt.

Here's a few quick recipes to get you started so that you can end that perfect meal.

'The basis of a good, tasty, healthy pudding is to avoid fat laden pastries or cream.'

Fruity Filo Baskets

Serves 4

Nutrition	per serving
Calories (kcal)	303.8
Carbohydrate (g)	63.0
Protein (g)	6.8
Fat (g)	3.5
Fibre (g)	3.3

Ingredients
4 sheets filo pastry, each cut into 4 squares
Low fat spray, to spray on sheets
100g carton low fat custard
50g low fat fromage frais
2 bananas, sliced
Handful of raspberries to garnish

Method
1. Line 4 patty tins, each with 4 filo pastry squares sprayed with low fat spray. Make sure each layer is covered with the spray (this makes the pastry crispy).
2. Place the cases into an oven set at 180°C/350°F/Gas Mark 4 for 5 minutes.
3. Combine the custard and fromage frais together, along with the chopped banana, and mix well.
4. Remove the pastry baskets from the oven and allow to cool.
5. Fill the individual baskets with the custard, fromage frais and banana mixture.
6. Decorate with raspberries.

Lemon & Lime Delight

Serves 4

Nutrition	per serving
Calories (kcal)	407.5
Carbohydrate (g)	53.3
Protein (g)	8.5
Fat (g)	17.0
Fibre (g)	1.4

Ingredients
1 x 22.5cm/9" flan base
1 packet lemon and lime jelly dissolved in 285ml boiling water
250g low fat fromage frais
Lemon rind twists (optional)

Method
1. Cut the sponge flan to a 9" diameter and place in a cake tin.
2. Dissolve the lemon-lime jelly in the boiling water. Leave to cool for an hour.
3. Combine the fromage frais and dissolved jelly together. Whisk until the mixture thickens.
4. Pour the mixture into the sponge base and refrigerate until it sets (roughly 2 to 3 hours).
5. Garnish with lemon twists.

Blueberry & Raspberry Muffins

Makes 8 - 10

Nutrition	per serving
Calories (kcal)	148.7
Carbohydrate (g)	25.4
Protein (g)	3.8
Fat (g)	3.6
Fibre (g)	0.8

A light and healthy sweet treat

Ingredients
200g plain flour
1 tbsp baking powder
Salt (pinch)
50g blueberries/raspberries
50g sugar
50g low fat margarine
1 beaten egg

Method
1. Preheat the oven to 200°C/400°F/Gas Mark 6.
2. Sift together the flour, baking powder and salt.
3. Add the blueberries/raspberries, gently folding into the dry ingredients.
4. Add the sugar and mix, forming a well in the centre of the mixture.
5. Melt the margarine in a small saucepan and then take off the heat.
6. Pour the beaten egg and melted margarine into the well and mix gently.
7. Spoon into paper muffin cases in a muffin pan and bake for 20 minutes.

Chocolate Muffins

Makes 8 - 10

Nutrition	per serving
Calories (kcal)	201.8
Carbohydrate (g)	29.9
Protein (g)	4.6
Fat (g)	7.3
Fibre (g)	0.8

Ingredients
200g plain flour
1 tbsp baking powder
Salt (pinch)
50g dark chocolate, chopped
50g caster sugar
50g low fat margarine
150ml single cream
1 beaten egg

Method
1. Preheat the oven to 200°C/400°F/Gas Mark 6.
2. Sift together the flour, baking powder and the salt. Add the chocolate pieces and mix all the ingredients together.
3. Add the sugar and mix, forming a well in the centre of the mixture.
4. Melt the margarine in a small saucepan and then take off the heat.
5. Pour in the cream, beaten egg and melted margarine into the well and mix gently.
6. Spoon into paper muffin cases in a muffin pan and bake for 20 minutes.

Baked Bananas

Serves 2

Nutrition	per serving
Calories (kcal)	188.0
Carbohydrate (g)	30.2
Protein (g)	1.4
Fat (g)	6.4
Fibre (g)	4.4

Ingredients
2 bananas
Juice of ½ orange
15g butter
1 tbsp brown sugar

Method
1. Preheat the oven to 220°C/425°F/Gas Mark 7.
2. Cut the bananas in half lengthways and lay in a baking dish.
3. Sprinkle with the juice of half an orange, put a knob of butter on each slice and sprinkle with brown sugar. Bake in the oven for 10 minutes and serve immediately.

Pancakes

Makes 12

Nutrition	per serving
Calories (kcal)	85.5
Carbohydrate (g)	7.8
Protein (g)	2.5
Fat (g)	5.0
Fibre (g)	0.2

Ingredients
115g plain flour
Salt (pinch)
2 eggs, beaten
4 tbsp sunflower margarine, melted
150ml whole milk and 150ml water mixed together

Method
1. Put the flour and salt in a bowl and form a well in the centre. Add the eggs, some of the milk and water and whisk in the flour, a little at a time.
2. Pour the rest of the liquid into the mixture, whisking until everything is mixed together.
3. Add half the melted margarine to the mixture and whisk again.
4. Using some of the margarine, brush the frying pan and heat until hot.
5. Pour in two tablespoons of the pancake mixture and tilt the pan from side to side until the pancake is spread thinly across the pan. Cook for a minute and then flip it over.
6. Serve with lemon juice or fresh fruit.

Flapjacks

Makes 9

Nutrition	per serving
Calories (kcal)	189.6
Carbohydrate (g)	23.4
Protein (g)	2.6
Fat (g)	9.6
Fibre (g)	2.2

Ingredients
50g raisins or sultanas
200g porridge oats
100g sunflower margarine
25g brown sugar
2 tbsp golden syrup

Method
1. Preheat the oven to 180°C/350°F/Gas Mark 4.
2. Lightly grease a small shallow (approx 9 x 7 inch) baking tin.
3. Put the raisins/sultanas and oats into a mixing bowl and stir until evenly mixed.
4. In a small saucepan, melt the margarine with the syrup and the sugar over a low heat. Add to the fruit and oats and mix well.
5. Turn the mixture into the greased tin and level the surface.
6. Bake for 20 - 30 minutes until a pale golden brown.
7. Leave in the tin until almost cold and then score into finger shapes with a sharp knife and loosen around the edges.
8. Remove from the tin to finish cooling on a wire rack. Eat immediately or store in an airtight container for up to a week.

Baked Apples

Serves 4

Nutrition	per serving
Calories (kcal)	317.6
Carbohydrate (g)	64.4
Protein (g)	5.4
Fat (g)	4.4
Fibre (g)	3.6

Ingredients
4 medium sized apples
50g raisins or sultanas
½ tsp cinnamon
2 tbsp brown sugar
25g low fat margarine
2 tbsp water
2 tbsp honey
Low fat custard to serve

Method
1. Preheat the oven to 190°C/375°F/Gas Mark 5. Wash and dry the apples and using a small sharp knife, make a shallow cut through the skin around the middle of each apple.
2. Core the apples and stand in an ovenproof dish.
3. Mix together the raisins/sultanas, cinnamon and sugar in a mixing bowl. Using a teaspoon, spoon the mixture into the centre of each apple and put a knob of margarine on each apple.
4. Pour the water and honey over the apples.
5. Bake the apples in the oven for 35 - 40 minutes or until tender and soft. Serve with low fat custard.

Strawberry Cheese

Serves 4

Nutrition	per serving
Calories (kcal)	92.9
Carbohydrate (g)	17.3
Protein (g)	5.4
Fat (g)	0.2
Fibre (g)	0.6

Ingredients
225g half fat fromage frais
25g caster sugar
2 tbsp strawberry jam
3 tbsp natural low fat yoghurt
225g strawberries

Method
1. Beat the fromage frais with the sugar and jam. Mix in the yoghurt.
2. Fold in the fruit and spoon into dishes.

Lemon Pudding

Serves 4

Nutrition	per serving
Calories (kcal)	271.4
Carbohydrate (g)	27.7
Protein (g)	7.4
Fat (g)	14.8
Fibre (g)	0.9

Ingredients
3 eggs, separated
50g sunflower margarine
75g caster sugar
Grated rind 1 lemon
Juice of 1 lemon
225ml whole milk
25g plain flour

Method
1. Preheat the oven to 180°C/350°F/Gas Mark 4. In a bowl beat the egg whites until stiff.
2. In a separate bowl, mix together the margarine and sugar until light and fluffy. Add the lemon rind, juice and egg yolks, one at a time, and beat in until well mixed. Beat in the milk, followed by the flour.
3. Fold the beaten egg whites into the lemon mixture and then pour into a greased ovenproof dish.
4. Put the dish in a roasting tin and pour hot water into the tin until it comes halfway up the sides of the dish. Bake in the oven for 35 minutes.
5. When served the pudding will have separated with a cake texture at the top and a sauce at the bottom.

Quick Fruity Crumble

Serves 4

Nutrition	per serving
Calories (kcal)	279.1
Carbohydrate (g)	63.8
Protein (g)	4.6
Fat (g)	1.5
Fibre (g)	7.2

Ingredients
2 large Bramley apples, peeled, cored and cut into pieces
50g blueberries, raspberries or blackberries
1 - 2 tbsp water
4 tbsp Demerara sugar
200g unsweetened muesli

Method
1. Preheat the oven to 190°C/375°F/Gas Mark 5.
2. Lightly grease an ovenproof dish with margarine.
3. Place the prepared apples and berries into the dish.
4. Pour in the water and sprinkle the sugar over the apples and berries.
5. Sprinkle muesli evenly over the apple and berry mixture and cover with a lid or foil.
6. Place into the oven and bake for 20 minutes, then remove lid/foil and continue baking for a further 15 - 20 minutes until lightly browned on top.

Summing Up

- Healthy puddings don't have to be boring.
- Get creative – fruit salads are not the only option.
- Avoid fat laden pastries or cream.
- Substitutes include fatless sponges, meringues, low fat fromage frais and yoghurt.

Chapter Nine

Entertaining

Cooking for someone special or just catering for your friends is a great way to practise your cooking skills and show them just how good you are in the kitchen. They might be pleasantly surprised! It's also a great way of making new friends in your first term.

The key to relaxing entertaining is to plan ahead of time so that everything runs smoothly without any hitches. You can then sit down with your friends and enjoy the party, rather than being stuck in the kitchen.

Getting the dinner party together

- Don't invite more people than can physically sit around your table (except if it's your family who will sit anywhere!). Also be aware that cooking for more than eight is a pain and doesn't work well – so forget it.

- When hosting a dinner party it's always a good idea to prepare ahead. Normally you would spend the whole day preparing but allow some time the day before for preparation.

- Write out a checklist and rough timetable and keep it taped up in the kitchen so that you can tick it off as you go. This keeps you calm and in control.

- Have a couple of dishes prepared in advance. A starter and pudding/dessert are the obvious ones, but you may only want to have one prepared instead.

- Stick to two or three courses, and no more. This cuts out a lot of last minute panic.

- Prepare dishes that you are familiar with and don't be too ambitious. Remember students will love any food you have prepared yourself.

'The key to relaxing entertaining is to plan ahead of time so that everything runs smoothly without any hitches. You can then sit down with your friends and enjoy the party, rather than being stuck in the kitchen.'

- Don't select a meal that leaves you with too much to do at the last minute.

- Check out whether you need extra glasses, plates or cutlery as you may need to borrow some from friends.

- Balance your planned menu with colour and texture. Don't double up on similar foods, for example fish as a starter and fish as a main course would be too much.

- Make sure your friends arrive about an hour before serving so that they can have pre-dinner drinks. Don't allow much more than an hour otherwise they become restless.

- Aim to have everything prepared well in advance before your friends arrive – setting up and decorating the table, setting out all the drinks, warming the plates, cleaning up the kitchen and getting everything ready for any last minute cooking that needs to be finished off.

Need2Know

Recipes

Green Chicken Stir-Fry

Serves 4

Nutrition	per serving
Calories (kcal)	332.7
Carbohydrate (g)	18.5
Protein (g)	31.9
Fat (g)	14.6
Fibre (g)	3.0

Ingredients
2 tbsp sunflower/olive oil
450g skinless chicken breasts, sliced into strips
2 cloves garlic, peeled and crushed
100g mange tout
1 large onion, sliced thinly
1 green pepper, seeded and sliced thinly
225g cabbage, washed and shredded
160g jar yellow bean sauce
3 tbsp cashew nuts

Method
1. Heat the oil in a non-stick wok or large frying pan.
2. Add the chicken and garlic to the pan and stir-fry for 5 minutes or until the chicken looks golden.
3. Add the mange tout, onion, pepper and cabbage to the pan. Stir-fry until the vegetables are tender.
4. Stir in the yellow bean sauce and heat for another 2 minutes.

5. Scatter the cashew nuts into the pan and mix well.
6. Serve with rice.

Mexican Chicken

Serves 4

Nutrition	per serving
Calories (kcal)	352.7
Carbohydrate (g)	22.8
Protein (g)	35.5
Fat (g)	13.3
Fibre (g)	3.1

Ingredients
3 tbsp sunflower/olive oil
4 skinless chicken breasts, chopped into cubes
1 medium onion, sliced thinly
2 cloves garlic, peeled and crushed
1 tbsp chilli powder
75g rice
340ml chicken/vegetable stock
Salt and pepper (optional)
3 tomatoes, chopped

Method
1. Heat the oil in a large non-stick frying pan over a high heat. Add the chicken and cook for 10 minutes until browned.
2. Add the onion, garlic, chilli powder and mix well. Reduce the heat to moderate and cook for 5 minutes.
3. Add the rice, stock, salt and pepper and cover. Cook for 25 minutes.
4. Add the tomatoes and stir. Cover and cook for a further 5 minutes.
5. Serve with a side salad.

Spicy Oriental Beef

Serves 4

Nutrition	per serving
Calories (kcal)	452.5
Carbohydrate (g)	7.3
Protein (g)	41.1
Fat (g)	28.9
Fibre (g)	2.7

Ingredients
700g steak, trimmed of fat and cut into thin slices
5 tbsp soy sauce
6 tbsp olive oil
2 large carrots, sliced into thin strips
4 sticks celery, sliced into thin strips
1 red pepper, seeded and sliced into thin strips
1 tsp ground ginger
½ tsp paprika
Salt (to taste)

Method
1. In a large bowl, combine the steak slices and soy sauce.
2. Heat half the oil in a non-stick frying pan for about 1 minute. Add the steak and cook for 5 minutes, stirring constantly so that the meat isn't pinkish. Once cooked, put the steak and juices into a separate bowl.
3. Heat the remaining oil in the same pan and add the carrots, celery, pepper, ginger and paprika. Cook, stirring for 3 minutes or until the vegetables are almost tender.
4. Reduce the heat and return the steak and juices to the pan. Simmer until heated through – about 2 minutes.
5. Serve with rice and salad.

Beef Casserole

Serves 4

Nutrition	per serving
Calories (kcal)	369.2
Carbohydrate (g)	11.9
Protein (g)	39.7
Fat (g)	18.5
Fibre (g)	2.5

Ingredients
1 tbsp flour
Salt and pepper (pinch)
675g stewing or braising steak, cubed
2 tbsp vegetable oil
2 medium onions, peeled and sliced thinly
2 carrots, sliced
1 tbsp tomato purée
1 clove garlic, peeled and crushed
Mixed herbs (pinch)
450ml beef stock

Method
1. Preheat the oven to 180°C/350°F/Gas Mark 4.
2. Mix the flour, salt and pepper on a plate. Lay the meat on top and ensure each piece is coated.
3. Heat a tablespoon of the oil in a casserole dish, fry the onions and carrots. Remove to a separate dish.
4. Heat the rest of the oil in the casserole dish, then add the meat and stir until the meat is brown all over.
5. Return the vegetables back to the dish with the meat. Add the tomato purée, garlic, herbs and stir.

6. Add the stock and stir. Put the lid on and cook in the oven for about 2 hours until the meat is tender.

Lentil & Sausage Stew

Serves 4

Nutrition	per serving
Calories (kcal)	723.5
Carbohydrate (g)	70.1
Protein (g)	39.7
Fat (g)	32.6
Fibre (g)	6.6

Ingredients
450g dried red lentils
2 tbsp vegetable/olive oil
1 medium onion, sliced thinly
1 clove garlic, peeled and crushed
1 x 400g can tomatoes
350g frankfurters (hot dog sausages), cut into slices
1 tbsp mixed herbs

Method
1. Preheat the oven to 200°C/400°F/Gas Mark 6. Rinse the lentils and put into a large saucepan. Cover with water, bring to the boil, cover with a lid and simmer for 20 minutes or until tender. Do not drain.
2. In another pan, heat the oil in a large non-stick pan and add the onions and garlic. Sauté until the onions are soft and stir in the tomatoes.
3. Pour the lentils and their cooking liquid into a large, greased casserole dish. Stir in the sausage, the tomato mixture and mixed herbs. Cover and bake for 20 minutes. Remove lid and bake for a further 5 minutes.
4. Serve with wholemeal, crusty rolls.

Low Fat Lasagne

Serves 6–8

Nutrition	per serving
Calories (kcal)	429.8
Carbohydrate (g)	35.2
Protein (g)	30.4
Fat (g)	18.8
Fibre (g)	3.1

Ingredients
1 ½ tbsp sunflower oil
2 medium onions, chopped
2 garlic cloves, peeled and crushed
450g lean minced beef
2 tbsp tomato purée
1 tsp basil
1 tsp thyme
150g mushrooms, sliced
1 x 400g can chopped tomatoes
1 ½ tsp salt
175ml beef stock
375g pre-cooked lasagne sheets
100g half-fat cheese, grated

White sauce
2 tbsp sunflower margarine
4 tbsp plain flour
350ml semi-skimmed milk, warmed

Method

1. Heat the oil in large non-stick pan, add the onions and sauté over a medium heat for 5 - 8 minutes.
2. Add the garlic and sauté for 1 minute and then add the meat. Cook the meat for 10 minutes until browned.
3. Add the tomato purée and cook for 2 - 3 minutes, then add the basil, thyme, mushrooms, salt and tomatoes. Cook for 5 minutes.
4. Pour in the stock, mix well and simmer for 10 minutes.
5. Make up the white sauce: melt the margarine in a pan, remove from the heat and add flour, mixing until smooth. Return the pan to the heat and cook for 2 minutes. Pour in the warmed milk and stir continuously until the sauce thickens. Remove from heat.
6. Using a large ovenproof rectangular dish that has been lightly greased, place a layer of the meat sauce in the dish. Place lasagne sheets on top followed by another layer of meat sauce. Repeat layering. The top layer should have lasagne sheets.
7. Pour over the white sauce and sprinkle the cheese on top.
8. Place in a preheated oven set at 180°C/350°F/Gas Mark 4 for 30 - 35 minutes.

Garlic Pork Steaks

Serves 6

Nutrition	per serving
Calories (kcal)	449.0
Carbohydrate (g)	7.3
Protein (g)	41.9
Fat (g)	28.1
Fibre (g)	1.2

Ingredients
1 ½ tbsp coriander seeds, crushed
2 garlic cloves, peeled and crushed
1 tsp salt
¼ tsp pepper
6 lean pork steaks
1 tbsp sunflower oil
200g mushrooms, sliced
200ml half-fat crème fraîche

Method
1. Preheat the oven to 150°C/300°F/Gas Mark 2.
2. Place the coriander seeds, garlic, salt and pepper into a small plastic bag and crush using a rolling pin.
3. Place the pork steaks into the bag, close and shake well so that the steaks are well seasoned.
4. Heat the oil in a large non-stick frying pan and add 3 steaks at a time, turning each until they are browned and place into an ovenproof dish. Add the remaining 3 and repeat.
5. Add the mushrooms to the pan and sauté for 3 – 4 minutes. Place into the ovenproof dish with the pork steaks.
6. Spoon the crème fraîche evenly over the pork steaks. Cover the dish and bake slowly for 45 minutes.

Need2Know

Narinder's Chicken Curry

Serves 6

Nutrition	per serving
Calories (kcal)	290.5
Carbohydrate (g)	7.2
Protein (g)	36.2
Fat (g)	13.1
Fibre (g)	1.4

Ingredients

25g butter or low fat sunflower spread
2 medium onions, chopped
½ tsp salt
1 tsp turmeric
3 garlic cloves, peeled and crushed
2 tsp ground ginger
8 chicken thighs, skin removed
¾ (400g) can chopped tomatoes
½ tsp cinnamon
3 - 4 green chillies, chopped finely with seeds left in

Method

1. Melt the butter/spread in a large non-stick saucepan, add the onions and salt. Sauté on a medium heat for 15 minutes.
2. When the water drains out from onions add the turmeric and sauté until browned.
3. Add the garlic and ginger and cook for a minute. Add the chicken thighs and cook for a further 5 - 8 minutes.
4. Add the chopped tomatoes, cover and cook for 20 - 25 minutes, then add the cinnamon.
5. Toss in the green chillies at the very end of cooking.
6. Serve with brown rice.

French Green Salad

Serves 6–8

Nutrition	per serving
Calories (kcal)	64.0
Carbohydrate (g)	5.0
Protein (g)	1.9
Fat (g)	4.1
Fibre (g)	1.4

Ingredients
1 garlic clove, peeled and cut in half
1 lettuce, core taken out, washed and torn into small pieces
4 spring onions, sliced
1 cucumber, sliced
1 green pepper, seeded and cut into rings
2 tomatoes, cut into wedges

French dressing
1 ½ tbsp olive oil
1 tbsp vinegar
¼ tsp salt
¼ tsp mustard
¼ tsp caster sugar

Method
1. Rub the garlic around a large serving dish and then throw away.
2. Arrange the lettuce leaves in a large bowl.
3. Add the spring onions, cucumber, green pepper and tomatoes to the bowl.
4. Mix together all the dressing ingredients in a jar/container and seal. Shake well and pour over the salad.
5. Toss lightly and serve.

Need2Know

Light Coleslaw

Serves 6–8

Nutrition	per serving
Calories (kcal)	84.1
Carbohydrate (g)	7.7
Protein (g)	2.8
Fat (g)	4.8
Fibre (g)	3.3

Ingredients

1 cabbage, sliced thinly
2 carrots, coarsely grated
2 celery sticks, sliced
1½ tsp salt
¼ tsp paprika
¼ tsp mustard
150g half-fat crème fraîche

Method

1. Place the cabbage, carrots and celery into a large bowl.
2. In a separate bowl mix together the salt, paprika, mustard and crème fraîche until well combined.
3. Pour the dressing over the vegetables, mix well, cover and chill in the fridge to develop flavour.

Apple & Pear Crumble

Serves 6 - 8

Nutrition	per serving
Calories (kcal)	427.1
Carbohydrate (g)	75.3
Protein (g)	5.0
Fat (g)	11.5
Fibre (g)	5.1

Ingredients
960g apples, peeled, cored and sliced
1 x 410g can of pears, drained
1 tsp ginger
2 tbsp brown sugar
2 tbsp water

Topping
175g plain flour
100g sunflower margarine
4 tbsp brown sugar
75g porridge oats
1 tsp vanilla essence

Method
1. Preheat the oven to 190°C/375°F/Gas Mark 5. Lightly grease a large ovenproof dish and arrange the prepared apples and pears.
2. Sprinkle over the ginger and sugar, and then pour the water evenly over the apples and pears.

3. In a large bowl, using your fingertips, rub together the plain flour and margarine until it resembles breadcrumbs. Add the sugar and oats, and mix well. Finally add the vanilla essence and mix together.
4. Spread the crumble mix evenly over the apple and pear mixture.
5. Place into the oven for 35 – 40 minutes.

Quick Fruity Whip

Serves 6–8

Nutrition	per serving
Calories (kcal)	143.9
Carbohydrate (g)	13.4
Protein (g)	8.7
Fat (g)	6.2
Fibre (g)	1.6

How to fan a strawberry

Using a sharp knife, cut the strawberry in half, keeping the stalk on. Make one cut into the bottom of the strawberry and the second cut just above. Finally, push the layers out slightly so they appear fanned.

Ingredients
25g sachet of sugar free raspberry/strawberry jelly
2 x 200ml cans evaporated milk, chilled
400g mixed fresh berries (strawberries, raspberries, blackberries), lightly crushed
8 large strawberries for decoration

Method
1. Dissolve the jelly crystals in 125ml boiling hot water and allow to cool.
2. Place the evaporated milk into a very large bowl and whisk until it thickens and doubles in size.
3. Add the cooled and dissolved jelly crystals and continue whisking until it is thoroughly mixed.
4. Add the lightly crushed fruit and mix.
5. Spoon into individual serving dishes and decorate with a fanned strawberry.

Posh Peaches

Serves 6–8

Nutrition	per serving
Calories (kcal)	359.6
Carbohydrate (g)	52.3
Protein (g)	5.8
Fat (g)	14.6
Fibre (g)	1.0

Suggestion – place a tablespoon of half-fat crème fraîche with each peach half, if desired.

Ingredients
1x 22.5cm/9" flan base, cut into 6 – 8 rounds using a medium scone cutter
4 tbsp peach juice or juice from the can of peaches
1 x 470g can peach halves, in natural fruit juice
8 scoops half-fat/light vanilla ice cream
4 tbsp raspberry sauce or coulis

Method
1. Place the flan rounds into individual serving dishes.
2. Spoon a little of the peach juice onto each sponge round and allow to soak.
3. Place a peach half into each sponge round and top with a scoop of ice cream.
4. Drizzle a teaspoon of raspberry sauce or coulis onto the ice cream.

Cooking for that special someone

A sure fire way of impressing a loved one or a possible future loved one is to cook them a special meal.

Pasta Arrabbiata

Serves 2

Nutrition	per serving
Calories (kcal)	524.1
Carbohydrate (g)	88.0
Protein (g)	18.0
Fat (g)	10.6
Fibre (g)	13.4

Ingredients
250g whole wheat pasta, cooked (see method on page 35)
1 tbsp olive oil
1 medium onion, chopped
1 clove garlic, peeled crushed
1 tsp hot chilli
1 tbsp tomato purée
125g canned tomatoes, chopped
125ml hot water
Salt and pepper (optional)

Method
1. While waiting for the pasta to cook, heat the oil in a large non-stick saucepan and sauté the onions for 6 - 8 minutes on a medium heat.
2. Add the garlic and cook for 1 - 2 minutes, add the chilli and cook for a further 2 minutes.
3. Add the tomato purée and cook for 5 minutes.
4. Pour in the chopped canned tomatoes and juice, followed by hot water. Stir and cook for 10 - 15 minutes until the liquid is reduced but not too thick.
5. Pour the sauce over the pasta and serve with a side salad.

Stir-Fry Spicy Pasta

Serves 2

Nutrition	per serving
Calories (kcal)	452.3
Carbohydrate (g)	52.0
Protein (g)	42.1
Fat (g)	8.3
Fibre (g)	9.0

Ingredients
150g cooked whole wheat penne or spirals (see method on page 35)
2 tsp olive/sunflower oil
2 skinless chicken breasts, cut into strips
1 garlic clove, peeled and chopped
1 chilli, finely chopped or ½ tsp powdered chilli
1 pepper, seeded and cut into medium pieces
¼ (400g) can chopped tomatoes
Salt and pepper (to season)

Method
1. While waiting for the pasta to cook, heat the oil in a large non-stick pan or wok and cook the chicken strips for 10 minutes.
2. Add the garlic and chilli and stir-fry for 2 - 3 minutes.
3. Toss in the pepper and cook for 5 minutes.
4. Add the chopped tomatoes and season with salt and pepper.
5. Stir through the cooked pasta and serve hot.

Pork Chops with Vegetables

Serves 2

Nutrition	per serving
Calories (kcal)	485.0
Carbohydrate (g)	38.9
Protein (g)	22.0
Fat (g)	27.1
Fibre (g)	4.6

Ingredients
1 tbsp vegetable oil
2 lean pork chops
110ml apple juice
60ml water
Salt and pepper (optional)
2 medium potatoes, scrubbed and sliced thinly
225g carrots, chopped
¼ tsp dried thyme
½ tbsp chopped parsley

Method
1. Heat the oil in a large non-stick frying pan over a moderately high heat for about 1 minute. Add the pork chops and cook for 4 minutes on each side until browned.
2. Add the apple juice, water, salt, pepper, potatoes, carrots, thyme and parsley. Cover and cook over a moderately low heat for 35 minutes or until the chops are tender and cooked through.

Need2Know

Spaghetti with Tuna & Tomatoes

Serves 2

Nutrition	per serving
Calories (kcal)	440.7
Carbohydrate (g)	60.4
Protein (g)	34.8
Fat (g)	6.9
Fibre (g)	4.0

Ingredients

225g spaghetti (use whole wheat if you want to be extra healthy)
25g low fat sunflower spread
1 clove garlic, peeled, finely chopped
3 tomatoes, peeled and chopped or 1 x small can tomatoes, chopped
1 x 185g can tuna, drained
Salt and pepper (to season)
1 ½ tbsp finely chopped parsley

Method

1. Cook the spaghetti (see method 35)
2. Melt the spread in a large non-stick frying pan over a low heat. Add the garlic and cook until golden. Add the tomatoes and cook for 10 minutes. Stir occasionally.
3. Add the tuna to the pan and stir. Cook for 5 minutes over a moderate heat. Remove from the heat and add salt, pepper and parsley. Mix well.
4. Drain the spaghetti and mix in with the sauce. Serve immediately.

Beef Chow Mein

Serves 2

Nutrition	per serving
Calories (kcal)	639.7
Carbohydrate (g)	35.4
Protein (g)	52.4
Fat (g)	32.8
Fibre (g)	7.8

Ingredients
1 tsp sunflower oil
1 medium onion, chopped
450g lean minced beef
1 tsp curry powder
2 celery sticks, sliced
¼ cabbage, sliced thinly
200g green beans
1 packet chicken soup mixed with 285ml water
50g Chinese noodles
Pepper (to season)

Method
1. Heat the oil in a non-stick wok or large saucepan and gently sauté the onions for 5 minutes over a medium heat.
2. Add the meat and fry for a further 5 minutes.
3. Add the curry powder and continue to fry for a further minute to develop the flavour.
4. Add the celery, cabbage and green beans. Cook for another 3 - 4 minutes.
5. Pour in the soup mix, noodles and pepper.
6. Cover the pan and bring to the boil, reduce the heat and simmer for 10 - 15 minutes. Serve immediately.

Festival Rice

Serves 2

Nutrition	per serving
Calories (kcal)	480.6
Carbohydrate (g)	52.0
Protein (g)	14.7
Fat (g)	25.0
Fibre (g)	5.1

Ingredients
1 carrot, coarsely grated
1 celery stick, sliced thinly
2 spring onions, sliced thinly
75g sultanas
40g pumpkin seeds, roasted
40g sunflower seeds, roasted
1 tsp soy sauce
2 tsp sunflower oil
2 tsp vinegar
2 tsp black pepper

Rice
125g brown rice, washed in a sieve and drained
¼ tsp salt
250ml boiling water

Method
1. Place the rice and salt in a small saucepan and add the water.
2. Place the lid on the saucepan and bring to the boil.

3. Once the pan is rapidly boiling, reduce the heat and simmer, take the lid off and continue to cook for 20 minutes or until the water has been absorbed and the rice is tender.
4. Replace the lid on the saucepan. Turn off the heat and allow the rice to stand for a further 5 minutes.
5. Place the rice, carrot, celery, onions and sultanas in a large bowl.
6. Add the pumpkin and sunflower seeds.
7. Whisk together the soy sauce, oil, vinegar and pepper.
8. Pour over the salad ingredients, mix and chill in the fridge.

Sweet & Sour Tofu kebabs

Serves 2

Nutrition	per serving
Calories (kcal)	203.1
Carbohydrate (g)	18.6
Protein (g)	15.9
Fat (g)	7.5
Fibre (g)	5.8

Ingredients
2 tbsp soy sauce
2 tbsp tomato sauce
1 tsp sunflower oil
¼ tsp chilli powder
¼ tsp salt
1/8 tsp pepper
1 garlic clove, crushed
1 courgette, sliced thickly
2 tomatoes, cut into quarters
1 medium onion, cut into quarters
1 pepper, seeded and cut into large pieces
8 button mushrooms
100g tofu, cut into cubes
Wooden skewers, soaked in water

Method
1. Combine the soy sauce, tomato sauce, sunflower oil, chilli, salt, pepper and crushed garlic into a large bowl. Mix well.
2. Add all the prepared vegetables and cubed tofu into the marinade. Gently mix so as not to break up the tofu. Allow to stand for 1 hour if possible so the flavours are developed.

3. Thread the vegetables alternately onto skewers. Place on a grill tray lined with aluminium foil and grill on a medium heat for 20 minutes or until cooked.

Chicken & Parma Ham Wraps

Serves 2

Nutrition	per serving
Calories (kcal)	335.5
Carbohydrate (g)	6.5
Protein (g)	48.6
Fat (g)	9.4
Fibre (g)	4.1

Ingredients
2 skinless chicken breasts
2 slices parma ham
2 tsp olive oil
1 clove garlic, peeled and chopped
1 leek, sliced thinly
200g mushrooms, wiped and sliced
100ml white wine
Salt and pepper (to taste)
2 cocktail sticks

Method
1. Preheat the oven to 180°C/350°F/Gas Mark 4.
2. Wash and prepare the chicken breasts, pat dry and wrap the parma ham around each breast and secure with a cocktail stick.
3. Heat the oil in a non-stick frying pan over a medium heat.
4. Place the chicken into the pan and cook gently for 8 - 10 minutes, turning until each side is browned. Remove from the pan and place into an ovenproof dish.
5. Add the garlic, leek and mushrooms to the frying pan and sauté for 3 minutes.
6. Pour in the wine and season with salt and pepper. Allow the wine to reduce to half the quantity.

7. Spoon this mixture over the chicken breasts and cover with a lid.
8. Place in the oven for 20 minutes.
9. Serve with boiled new potatoes and steamed green beans.

Salmon Tropicana

Serves 2

Nutrition	per serving
Calories (kcal)	340.4
Carbohydrate (g)	10.6
Protein (g)	31.6
Fat (g)	19.0
Fibre (g)	1.4

This dish is not only low fat and tasty but is also a refreshing change from the usual rich and fatty sauces served with salmon.

Ingredients
1 tbsp black peppercorns, crushed
1 tbsp lemon juice
2 salmon fillets
1 tsp olive/sunflower oil

Lime yoghurt
125g natural low fat yoghurt
1 tsp honey
1 tbsp fresh chives, chopped
1 tbsp lime juice
1 tsp lime rind, finely grated

Method
1. In a small bowl, combine the yoghurt, honey, chives, lime juice and rind. Mix well and chill in the fridge.
2. Place the peppercorns and lemon juice in a freezer bag. Add the salmon fillets and shake well. Marinate for 5 minutes.

3. Heat the oil in a non-stick frying pan over a medium heat and add the salmon fillets. Cook for 3 – 4 minutes on each side. If the flesh flakes, it's cooked.
4. Serve the salmon fillets with a dollop of lime yoghurt on top.

Chocolate Dipped Strawberries

Serves 2

Nutrition	per serving
Calories (kcal)	224.1
Carbohydrate (g)	29.6
Protein (g)	3.5
Fat (g)	10.3
Fibre (g)	4.8

Ingredients
75g dark chocolate, broken up into small pieces or use chocolate chips
300g strawberries

Method
1. Line a flat baking sheet with baking paper.
2. Place water into a small saucepan, bring to the boil and simmer.
3. Place the chocolate into a small bowl and place over the simmering water so that the chocolate melts. Do not let the water boil.
4. Dip each strawberry into the chocolate, swirling it around so that only half of the strawberry is coated. When coated, place them on the lined baking sheet and put in the fridge for 10 minutes to set.

Black Cherry Fool

Serves 2

Nutrition	per serving
Calories (kcal)	84.0
Carbohydrate (g)	16.9
Protein (g)	4.1
Fat (g)	0.2
Fibre (g)	0.2

This is a very quick and easy pudding recipe.

If you're not keen on black cherry use canned apple and blackberry filling instead.

Ingredients
100g fat free fromage frais
100g canned black cherry filling

Method
1. Place the fromage frais into a medium bowl.
2. Add the black cherry filling and fold through with a large spoon. For swirls of colour, try not to completely mix the ingredients.
3. Spoon the mixture into glasses and chill in the fridge.

Cooking for crowds

At some point in your student life you'll have a party catering for the masses. It's a good idea not to use top quality serving dishes and opt for small plastic bowls instead to avoid breakages. Always have some food in reserve and don't put all the food out at once so that late party people have something to munch on.

Catering food guide

Estimating the amount of food you need in catering for a crowd is daunting for experienced cooks, let alone someone who isn't. A lot of food and money can be wasted if you don't get it right. Here's a guide that can help you overcome the stumbling blocks.

Food	1 portion	24-26 people
Chicken pieces	75g – 100g	2 – 3kg
Sliced ham/chicken	75g – 100g	2 – 3.5kg
Low fat pate	25g – 50g	1.5kg
Lettuce	1/6	3 to 4
Cucumber	2cm	3 to 4
Tomatoes	1 to 2	1.5kg
Boiled potatoes	50g	1.5kg
Cabbage	25g	1.5kg
Rice or pasta	40g (uncooked)	1.2kg
Low fat cheese (on biscuits)	25g – 30g	1/2 kg – 1.5kg
Dried biscuits		1 kg

Quick garnishes

Food always looks its best when it's presented with small touches and shows that you've made an effort. Here are a few ideas you might want to use when presenting your dishes.

Orange and lemon twists

Slice an orange or lemon thinly (but not too thin). Slit through the slice to the rind then right through to the centre. Twist the slice in the opposite direction. You can also double them up using two slices. This looks very effective, especially on platters of food.

Spring onions

Trim off the root and most of the green leaves. Slit the onions down the stem and leave in icy, cold water so that they curl. These curls look fabulous on meat, savoury or open sandwich platters.

Ridged cucumber slices

Drag a metal fork along the full length of the cucumber all the way around, creating ridges. Slice very thinly. These slices can be used around the edges of platters.

Vegetable curls

Using a vegetable peeler, peel downwards or around the fruit or vegetable so that you're left with one long piece. Using your fingers twist the vegetable or fruit strip, starting in the centre so that it forms a flower.

Summing Up

▨ Cooking for your friends or someone special doesn't need to be stressful.

▨ Plan ahead and get orgnanised-don't leave everything to the last minute!

▨ Balance your planned menu with colour and texture.

Help List

Organisations

British Nutrition Foundation (BNF)

High Holborn House, 52 – 54 High Holborn, London, WC1V 6RQ
Tel: 0207 4046504
www.nutrition.org.uk
The BNF promotes the wellbeing of society through the interpretation and dissemination of scientifically based knowledge and advice on the relationship between diet, exercise and health.

Department of Health

Richmond House, 79 Whitehall, London, SW1A 2NS
Tel: 0207 2104850
www.dh.gov.uk/en/Publichealth/Healthimprovement/index.htm
Provides information on health improvement through food, including details on tackling obesity, maintaining a healthy lifestyle through diet and nutrition and the 5 -a-day programme.

Food Standards Agency (FSA)

Aviation House, 125 Kingsway, London, WC2B 6NH
Tel: 0207 2768829
www.food.gov.uk
www.eatwell.gov.uk
The Food Standards Agency is an independent government department set up by an Act of Parliament in 2000 to protect the public's health and consumer interests in relation to food. They cover all areas of food and the website contains lots of useful and interesting information.

NHS Direct

Riverside House, 2A Southwark, Bridge Road, London, SE1 9HA
Tel: 0845 4647
www.nhsdirect.nhs.uk
NHS Direct provides 24-hour health care, delivering telephone and e-health information services day and night direct to the public. They have quizzes, FAQ's and more information related to diet and eating.

Books and leaflets

1001 Little Healthy Eating Miracles

By Esme Floyd, Carlton Books Ltd, London, 2008.

E for Additives

By Maurice Hanssen and Jill Marsden, Thorsons, London, 1987.

Food: Healthy Eating (Go Facts)

By Paul McEvoy, A & C Black Publishers Ltd, London, 2006.

The Healthy Heart Diet Book (Positive Health Guide)

By Roberta Longstaff, Optima, London, 1988.

Nutrition For Dummies (UK Edition) (Paperback)

By Nigel Denby, Sue Baic, Carol Ann Rinzler, John Wiley & Sons, London, 2005.

Which Way to a Healthier Diet

By Judy Byrne, "Which?" Consumer guides, Penguin Books, London, 1994.

'Eight Guidelines for a Healthy Diet'
'Understanding Food Labels'
'About Food Additives and Food Safety'

All available from the Department of Health, Food Sense, London, SE99 7TT. Tel. 0208 8862.

Websites

www.bbc.co.uk/food/news_and_events/events_student1.shtml
This BBC website provides information for new students. Includes smart shopping tips, budget advice and recipes.

www.hss.uk.net/ADVERT
This site features the portable halogen power oven which is the healthier way to cook. Very useful for students and worth exploring.

www.studentcook.co.uk
Student Cook was formed to offer a unique reference point on student cooking for all occasions and budgets. The website includes tips on preparing, cooking, eating, storing and shopping for food. Information on shopping to a budget and healthy eating is included.

www.studentguru.co.uk/studentsurvival/student-cooking
Packed with lots of healthy recipes, this website is well worth a visit. You can also find information on other student issues such as accommodation, jobs and finance.

www.yumyum.com/student
This is a free recipe website for everyday cooks, including information for students. Lots of useful tips and advice, so well worth a visit!

In Conclusion

Hopefully this book will help you to understand the basics of healthy eating and inspire you to use this nutritional information in a positive way. You'll feel the benefits within days, not only will you look good but energy levels and focus in getting through your studies will greatly improve. By following the quick and easy recipes you'll be on your way towards eating for a healthier life.

Weight Loss Resources

Nutritional information was supplied and verified by Weight Loss Resources Ltd. For further help and information with healthy eating and nutrition, please visit www.weightlossresources.co.uk.

Need - 2 - Know

Available Titles Include ...

Allergies A Parent's Guide
ISBN 978-1-86144-064-8 £8.99

Autism A Parent's Guide
ISBN 978-1-86144-069-3 £8.99

Blood Pressure The Essential Guide
ISBN 978-1-86144-067-9 £8.99

Dyslexia and Other Learning Difficulties
A Parent's Guide ISBN 978-1-86144-042-6 £8.99

Bullying A Parent's Guide
ISBN 978-1-86144-044-0 £8.99

Epilepsy The Essential Guide
ISBN 978-1-86144-063-1 £8.99

Your First Pregnancy The Essential Guide
ISBN 978-1-86144-066-2 £8.99

Gap Years The Essential Guide
ISBN 978-1-86144-079-2 £8.99

Secondary School A Parent's Guide
ISBN 978-1-86144-093-8 £9.99

Primary School A Parent's Guide
ISBN 978-1-86144-088-4 £9.99

Applying to University The Essential Guide
ISBN 978-1-86144-052-5 £8.99

ADHD The Essential Guide
ISBN 978-1-86144-060-0 £8.99

Student Cookbook – Healthy Eating The Essential Guide
ISBN 978-1-86144-069-3 £8.99

Multiple Sclerosis The Essential Guide
ISBN 978-1-86144-086-0 £8.99

Coeliac Disease The Essential Guide
ISBN 978-1-86144-087-7 £9.99

Special Educational Needs A Parent's Guide
ISBN 978-1-86144-116-4 £9.99

The Pill An Essential Guide
ISBN 978-1-86144-058-7 £8.99

University A Survival Guide
ISBN 978-1-86144-072-3 £8.99

View the full range at **www.need2knowbooks.co.uk**.
To order our titles call **01733 898103**, email **sales@ n2kbooks.com** or visit the website. Selected ebooks available online.

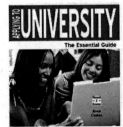
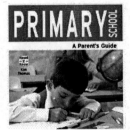

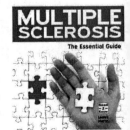

Need - 2 - Know, Remus House, Coltsfoot Drive, Peterborough, PE2 9BF